RELEVANCY

by LINKED IN AND TOWN HALL ACHIEVER OF THE YEAR
EY NOMINEE ENTREPRENEUR OF THE YEAR
GRAND HOMAGE LYS DIVERSITY

Dr. BAK NGUYEN, DMD

&

by TWO TIMES LAUREATE IOOI WORLD CONGRESS TOP PRESENTER
WORLD'S TOP 100 DOCTORS IN DENTISTRY

Dr. PAUL OUELLETTE, DDS, MS, ABO, AFAAID

guest authors

Dr. ANIL GUPTA
Dr. PAUL DOMINIQUE
Dr. ERIC LACOSTE

Dr. NACH DANIEL
Dr. JULIO CESAR REYNAFARJE
Dr. MARIA KUNSTADTER
Dr. DUC-MINH LAM-DO
Dr. JEREMY KRELL
Dr. AGATHA BIS

MARTIN LAVALLÉE
ALIA ALAOUI
JONAS DIOP

TO ALL THOSE RELATED IN THE DENTAL INDUSTRY ,
DOCTORS, HYGIENISTS, ASSISTANTS, DENTURISTS, SECRETARIES,
SALES PEOPLE, TECHNICIANS, DENTAL EXECUTIVES, INVESTORS, PATIENTS, WE
ARE ALL IN THE SAME BOAT. IT IS TIME TO ACT AS ONE.

by Dr. BAK NGUYEN
& Dr. PAUL OUELLETTE

Copyright © 2020 Dr. BAK NGUYEN

All rights reserved.

ISBN: 978-1-989536-39-1

ABOUT THE AUTHORS

From Canada, **Dr Bak Nguyen**, Nominee EY Entrepreneur of the year, Grand Homage LYS DIVERSITY, and LinkedIn & TownHall Achiever of the year. Dr Bak is a cosmetic dentist, CEO and founder of Mdex & Co. His company is revolutionizing the dental field. Speaker and motivator, he wrote more than 65 books in 2 years and a half, accumulating many world records (to be officialized).

From USA: **Dr. Paul Ouellette**, DDS, MS, ABO, AFAAID, WORLD TOP 100 DENTISTS, Former Associate Professor Georgia School of Orthodontics and Jacksonville University. A visionary man looking for the future of our profession. Dr. Paul Ouellette Highly motivated to help my sons become successful in the "Ouellette Family of Dentists" Group Dental Specialty Practice.

GUEST AUTHORS

From USA: **Dr. Anil Gupta** is a world-class speaker and coach helping people to find their purpose and happiness. Dr. Gupta is in the quest to improve one billion lives throughout the world. A man of wisdom, a kind force of nature and a motivator spreading hope.

From USA, **Dr. Paul Dominique** is a pediatric dentist who joined the profession at 27 years old. From public dental health, he moved on to build a network of clinics and sold them a few years back. Now, at 49, he is half retired and is investing in different dental tech companies, including teledentistry.

From Canada, **Dr Eric Lacoste**, Periodontist and MBA, Dr Lacoste is a community leader and great entrepreneur who is fighting for the weakest links of our society, especially children. Twice DUNAMIS laureate, HOMAGE from the Quebec Dentists Order and winner of the TELUS Social Implication Award.

From Canada, **Dr. Nach Daniel** is an Oral & Maxillofacial Surgeon and successful businessman with more than 300 employees in his dental company, EAST COAST DENTAL GROUP. Dr. Daniel has a diverse portfolio ranging from commercial real estate to AI.

From USA, **Dr. Maria Kunstadter**, Doctor of Dental Surgery, co-founder THE TELEDENTIST, the biggest TELEDENTISTRY provider in USA. Experienced President with a demonstrated history of working in the hospital & health care industry. Skilled in Customer Service, Sales, Strategic Planning, Team Building, and Public Speaking. Strong business development professional with a Doctor of Dental Surgery focused in Advanced General Dentistry from UMKC School of Dentistry.

From Peru: **Dr. Julio Reynafarje**, dentist, Dean of the Peruvian Dental Association postgraduate School of continued Education. Postgraduate professor for more than 15 years, with more than 100 international lectures and with publications in many languages in magazines worldwide, he is also the author of the book Sfumato in Esthetic dentistry and is an active entrepreneur in Medical issues.

From Canada, **Dr Duc-Minh Lam-Do**, dentist for 16 years with a practice emphasis on functional and physiologic dentistry, co-founder of teledentistes.com, the first teledentistry platform in Quebec. He is the founder of the Montreal Tongue-tie Institute, the first comprehensive multidisciplinary center for the treatment of ankyloglossia for babies, children and adults who have issues related with breastfeeding, swallowing, breathing, speech and craniofacial growth. He is one of 6 dentists in Quebec who has a mastership from the American Academy of Dental Sleep Medicine.

From USA, **Dr Jeremy Krell**, dentist MBA and serial entrepreneur, the real definition of an OVERACHIEVER. Highly experienced innovator and entrepreneur with a proven track record of taking early-stage startups to acquisition (multi-million dollar buyout). Excellent clinical dentistry and communication skills with in-depth analytical, organizational, and problem-solving abilities. A detail orientated and strategic leader in a dynamic, expeditious innovative environment. Firm experience with strategy, positioning companies, leading & developing teams, raising capital, investor relations, dental materials & techniques, negotiating & closing deals, and sales.

From Canada, **Dr. Agatha Bis**, dentist for 20 years+, founder of UPB Dental Academy.

From Canada: **Martin Lavallée, MBA**, and CEO of the INSTITUT DENTAIRE INTERNATIONAL (I.D.I) dedicated to accompany and support with continuous education the dentists on their journey to excel.

From Canada: **Alia Alaoui,** CEO of SWIPELIST Inc., Artificial intelligence marketplace that connects patients with dentists

From France, **Jonas Diop**, coach and podcaster, Jonas is the voice of a new generation, one refusing to bow down to anything less than life to the fullest. Entrepreneur and businessman, his passion is to empower the dreamer within each individual to become achievers. From dreamer to achiever!

RELEVANCY

by Dr. BAK NGUYEN
& Co-Author Dr. PAUL OUELLETTE

GUEST AUTHORS

Dr. ANIL GUPTA
Dr. PAUL DOMINIQUE
Dr. ERIC LACOSTE
Dr. NACH DANIEL
Dr. JULIO CESAR REYNAFARJE
Dr. MARIA KUNSTADTER
Dr. DUC-MINH DO-LAM
Dr. JEREMY KRELL
Dr. AGATHA BIS
MARTIN LAVALLÉE
ALIA ALAOUI
JONAS DIOP

INTRODUCTION
BY Dr. BAK NGUYEN

A LEADER HAS A BIG HEART
CHAPTER 1 - Dr. PAUL OUELLETTE

BUILDING FROM THE DIFFERENCE
CHAPTER 2 - Dr. BAK NGUYEN

THE OUELLETTE INITIATIVE
CHAPTER 3 - Dr. PAUL OUELLETTE

THE VOID
CHAPTER 4 - Dr. BAK NGUYEN

THE HAPPINESS FORMULA
CHAPTER 5 - Dr. ANIL GUPTA

ON THE OTHER SIDE
CHAPTER 6 - Dr. BAK NGUYEN

THE JOY OF GIVING
CHAPTER 7 - Dr. PAUL OUELLETTE

HUMILITY, FLEXIBILITY AND ADAPTABILITY
CHAPTER 8 - Dr. BAK NGUYEN

LOOKING AT THE PAST TO GLIMPSE THE FUTURE
CHAPTER 9 - Dr. PAUL DOMINIQUE

DO IT BECAUSE YOU CAN
CHAPTER 10 - Dr. BAK NGUYEN

THE OUELLETTE LEGACY
CHAPTER 11 - Dr. PAUL OUELLETTE

THE TIME FOR HALF MEASURES IS OVER
CHAPTER 12 - Dr. BAK NGUYEN

THE DOMINIQUE INITIATIVE
CHAPTER 13 - Dr. PAUL DOMINIQUE

3% RELEVANCY
CHAPTER 14 - Dr. BAK NGUYEN

THE LACOSTE INITIATIVE
CHAPTER 15 - Dr. ERIC LACOSTE

A NEW WORLD DIALOGUE
CHAPTER 16 - Dr. BAK NGUYEN

REINVENTING ONESELF
CHAPTER 17 - Dr. PAUL OUELLETTE

PART II

AN OPEN DIALOGUE
CHAPTER 18 - Dr. BAK NGUYEN

THE PACE OF CHANGE
CHAPTER 19 - Dr. NACH DANIEL

FACING THE FACTS
CHAPTER 20 - Dr. MARIA KUNSTADTER

HATIKVAH
CHAPTER 21 - Dr. JEREMY KRELL

THE IMPORTANCE OF BEING A GAME-CHANGER
CHAPTER 22 - Dr. JULIO CESAR REYNAFARJE

LIGHTNING BOLT
CHAPTER 23 - ALIA ALAOUI

THE OPPORTUNITY TO REGROUP
CHAPTER 24 - MARTIN LAVALLÉE

I AM A FIXER
CHAPTER 25 - Dr. AGATHA BIS

I AM DENTIST
CHAPTER 26 - Dr. DUC-MINH DO-LAM

AN ALPHA
CHAPTER 27 - JONAS DIOP

CONCLUSION
by Dr. BAK NGUYEN

INTRODUCTION
by Dr. BAK NGUYEN

I am still in the midst of **THE GREAT PAUSE**, a forced pause. Even if it is called that so, it is not a pause, at least not to me. I have never worked as hard in my entire career as a dentist, even now that my clinic is shutdown and confined at home. Why is that? Because I refused to lay down and lose, because I reinvented myself.

That was my only way to keep depression away and to find some rationality and sanity. It was my way to keep my relevancy. I went out, took my iPhone, my camera and my laptop to setup where I was still allowed to travel, the only place virus-free, the web.

I reached out to profiles and names, names that I never met nor talk to in real life, asking how they were doing and seeking their perspective on the events at hand. It is then that I noticed that all of the world was looking in the same direction, in a giant void, in denial.

We were all under pressure and much stresses. Some amongst us have been called to the front, to fight, at the forefront, an invisible enemy that most of us did not even believe was a threat until lately. Forced into inactivity and confinement, we all obeyed, leaving behind most of our lives and skills and expertise. Those are the facts.

> "We were left with all of our abilities
> and one great gift: TIME!"
> Dr. Bak Nguyen

Refusing to stay idle or to let depression take over, I raised up. I wasn't alone. Some raised their voices and proposed to conscript at the front line, adapting their skills to serve at their best. Some others were vexed left behind, not mobilized and valued in the war effort. Some others, like myself, decided to prepare for the **AFTERMATH**, the second wave of this war, the recession.

Left with my abilities and the gift of **TIME**, I decided to mobilized and to rally in order to face the next menace, one that is much more devastating and that will affect, not a percentage of the population, but all of the world population.

At the same time, I was reminded by my team, patients and own wounds how unequipped and unprepared my industry (dental) was facing will be following: **THE REBOOT**.

That's how I meant Paul, online. He was the first person to respond back to me and genuinely accepted my invitation for an interview online to share his perspective of the new world order and the place of our profession in it.

Strangely, he did not seem depressed, hopeless or even stressed. He was worried, but he was also genuinely calm and hopeful: he now has time! From a random encounter, we connected through a tele-interview, exchanging and discussing on what our profession will be facing next and how it might die, adapt or become irrelevant. A few days later, I had a plan to relaunch our industry.

Before this crisis, I was about to launch the second phase of the deployment of **Mdex & Co**, changing the world from a dental chair. As the infrastructures were in place and the expansion began, I was about to launch seminars and online coaching to teach dentists to become millionaires.

Yup, for 2 years, I tried to explain how to be happier, free and efficient, but every time, people we more responsive to my wealth, power and confidence. I had to listen to my market, so I adapted my wording and message to give them what they wanted. Still happiness and freedom but packaged within a word that they all understood without too much explanation: millionaire.

That's how, since the beginning of the year, my team and I worked on the launch of a new brand, **THE ALPHAS**. I was about to launch my master class and seminars when I received the directive to close shop and to stay home.

Going online and connecting, I needed a brand so people could identify and relate too. I took what was available and right within reach: **THE ALPHAS**. From an elite organization of the wealthy, overachievers and top performers, it became the rallying point of the thinkers and those looking forward to save our profession and the economy.

Curiously enough, those looking forward are all overachievers, top performers and wealthy people. There was no selection, they sorted themselves from responding to the events and to my call. Within days, I had around me **ALPHAS** from different industries, from different countries and especially, the **ALPHA DENTISTS** looking to win for more than themselves.

This is how my friendship with Paul started. "A brother from another mother" is how he addressed me, a few days after our encounter. He could have been my dad, my teacher and mentor, instead, we were friends and partner in the new endeavor, one to lead our industry to safe shores.

Is this the fabulation of two people bored in confinement? Look for yourself how our work has contributed to awake our industry and how **THE ALPHAS** have drafted the first steps of the rebuilding. Dr. Paul Ouellette is at the center of **THE OUELLETTE** initiative, a way to resume our line of duty with patients in our chairs and fixing , at the same time, our lack of social implication in society as an industry.

Can our lack of implication be debated? Look at how our profession is perceived by the general population and you will find a clear answer: expensive, unfriendly and often greedy! Except in France, over there, dentists are elected in mayor's office!

From France to USA, from Peru to Canada, **THE ALPHAS** were coming from everywhere. At the time of this writing, many big corporations of the industry have reached out to offer their help and support to our initiative.

So this is the journey, the motivation and the reason for our fight: one against **complacency**, **ignorance** and **denial**. Both Paul and I hate confrontation, but we are not scared of looking the enemy in the eye and not backing down. Well, this time, there is no enemy, just a void and some bad habits to lay down!

Very far from our training and professional habit, we are not looking to be perfection, to establish the next protocol or to impose our views. That rigid state of mind looking for perfection and standardization led us where we are today.

On the contrary, we are looking to connect with all those with ideas and the desire to voice up. Even if their opinions are opposite to ours, we will be listening. Actually, I will even be giving them the floor to speak, if they have at heart the better future of the collective.

Much more than another self-proclaimed intellectual elite group, we are nothing but the first who join. Our trade is dynamic and humility. The dynamic to never settle and the humility to seek for more, for better, even if we know some.

In the first part of this book, you'll be reading from Paul and myself, two individuals from two generations, from two different countries. But very soon, other Alphas will be joining to share with you their perspectives. Relevancy is not a straight forward narrative, but a dialogue and a dance in the hope to find strong footing for each of us, and hopefully, each of you.

This is our wording and spirit. It is of uttermost importance for the survival and relevancy of or kind, dental professionals. And by dental professionals, I included doctors, hygienists, assistants, technician, executive, secretary, denturist, sale and marketing people, we are all together in this. It is time to act as one.

> "This the renewal, one base on friendship beyond borders, age and prejudices."
> **Dr. Bak Nguyen**

This is how we will prevail. This is how we will all survive. This is how we will prosper, as one. This is **RELEVANCY**.

> In times of crisis,
> It is the perfect opportunity
> To reinvent who we are.
>
> **Dr. BAK NGUYEN**

CHAPTER 1
"A LEADER HAS A BIG HEART"
by Dr. PAUL OUELLETTE

It's been about a month before this writing when I first met a Canadian "Rockstar" Dentist, Dr. Bak Nguyen. He contacted me out of the blue one day. I was in week two of self-isolation with my family in Saint Augustine, Florida. The **CV-19 Pandemic** changed everything for my family and the world a few weeks earlier.

In isolation, I knew that I would probably surrender to boredom and laziness as I could now sleep in, read a few books and binge Netflix. How boring was that perspective ahead! Dr. Bak got me out of my boredom. For that, I am forever grateful.

You, see, I am someone who can hardly take vacations, a staycation for more than 3 to 4 days, that's the best I could enjoy. Now, forced into confinement, I can't see the light through this one. I inherited the workaholic trait from my dear mother. She is going to be 97 years old this September. Lanette Ouellette is the patriarch of our family!

She raised my brother and I and all our grandchildren to be givers. She was very active in our local Florida community and easily made friends with EVERYONE no matter their status, race or age.

She has a standing record for recruiting more **Rotarians** in her Indian Harbour Beach Chapter than any other member during her service to the organization. She served as a member or eventually as president of many local organizations.

She had the honor to sit with President Reagan and Senator Nelson at a community event when they visited the **NASA Space Center**. I proudly display the picture of them in my study. Our family members all learned how to give back to the community from Lanette. She instilled the **Joy of Giving** in everyone, friends and family.

> "A brother from another mother."
> Dr. Paul Ouellette

Dr. Bak, my brother from another mother, as I dearly call him, talked to me for a few minutes that day. Bak asked me to participate in an online interview with him that Friday. He wanted to hear my opinions and perspective about the Future of Dentistry post-pandemic.

I happily accepted his invitation and continued to do a little pre-interview research about what other colleagues were predicting. I am a member of several online dental and medical blog groups.

There are many opinions and great suggestions for how to get through this world-changing event. I DO NOT have all the answers! However, I'll gladly use my 50 years of experience in dentistry, pass on other people's comments, share ideas and put my spin on it.

> "To listen before opening."
> Lanette Ouellette

There are so many intelligent, caring, sharing and serial givers in our profession. The pandemic has brought out the best in all of our friends and colleagues. To get through this "Speed Bump" we can now work together and stop competing for a while.

After the first Alphas online interview with Bak, we got along naturally, just like this was meant to be. I must admit, I had much fun sharing with him. Never would I have expected of what would come next. A few days after, I received in my inbox a notification telling me to go online.

I went and discovered a wonderful video with my name tagged on the post. Bak was hosting a 7-8 minutes video mapping the troubles that we were in, as a society and as an industry. I saw many names and different leaders interviewed. But more than mapping our present, Bak was putting the pieces together and was inviting the profession to rally and to work toward a solution. He called those people **THE ALPHAS**.

What was an interview to me, became a masterplan under his care, Bak's care. I was featured and named. Being an **OUELLETTE** and under the leadership of Lanette, our patriarch, I am a **GIVER**. **ALPHAS** works for me! That's how I came onboard. A few email exchanges, a phone call and I was part of the initiative to save our industry, the dental industry. I was now part of **THE ALPHA**'s initiative.

The first initiative was to find a way for dentists all around the world to resume their duties, even in confinement. Technology was our solution. The first topic was TeleDentistry. Bak offered me a seat at the table of panelists. Of course, I accepted!

Our family has a long history of using technology in our practices. In 2010, we developed a free online iPhone App, **BracesHelp** V2.3 (iBracesHelp2010-V1). We have had more than 80,000 downloads since its launch. One of the Apps features allowed our patients to use their iPhone to take an image of an orthodontic problem and send it to us via the **BracesHelp** App.

Current TeleDentistry and TeleMedicine applications have greatly improved and expanded the use of today's online connectivity. The future of medicine and dentistry will use this technology to save patients time and protect us all, patients and caregivers, from future exposure to pathogens such as CV-19 and others.

I was happy to be of use and contributing for ways to look ahead. A few more emails and calls, I introduced Bak to some of the greatest dental minds and thinkers I had the privilege to know. Dr. Robert Boyd, an orthodontist and periodontist part of the team leading the digitalization and democratization of orthodontics a few years ago.

Dr. Paul Dominique, a pediatric dentist who owned several clinics and had invested into a company providing TeleDentistry in the USA. There were a few more leaders, but those are the one who got along with Bak and accepted to join the first **INTERNATIONAL DENTAL SUMMIT** by **THE ALPHAS**.

I contributed and participated in an online summit the following week with a panel of **Dental Thought Leaders** on the subject of TeleDentistry, our first initiative. I have to say how impressed I was of the other leaders on board.

What I thought was marketing and labels, branding a webinar as **INTERNATIONAL** was, in fact, a true summit with a dentist and mayor in France, Dr. Philippe Fau, speaking French in the summit with Bak, and Dr. Eric Lacoste, a periodontist standing in for Canada. Really, I was open, but now, I was excited to be part of a world community.

Earlier this year, I received the award and honor to be recognized as one of the **world TOP 100 dentists**. I humbly accepted… but since nothing comes of nothing, things were starting to make sense to me. The stars were aligned for this, for us to make a difference and to lead our profession back on track.

This is how it started, not the virus, but the solution. We, **OUELLETTES** are people of solutions and **GIVERS**. This is how I proudly became an **ALPHA**.

This is how we will prevail. This is how we will all survive. This is how we will prosper, as one. This is **RELEVANCY**.

Dr. BAK NGUYEN

CHAPTER 2
"BUILDING FROM THE DIFFERENCE."
by Dr. BAK NGUYEN

a tribute to my friend and mentor, Dr. Jean De Serres.

Six years ago, I woke up feeling that my country was under threat by unilateral views and authoritarian political leaders. I stood up, suited up and got ready for a fight. From a dentist, I emerge as what people did not expect. I surprised everyone and rallied unusual partners.

I got offered to run for office, and I declined. It is not the first time that I declined such an invitation. Don't get me wrong, I am flattered, but for as long as there is someone else who could do the job, please give it to that person. I am a lazy guy, genuinely lazy! That being said, if no one is standing up, it falls to my shoulder to do it.

That's what I did helping a health crisis in my province shortly after the political victory, even if I didn't run. I got the negotiation moving further and faster in a month than it was for the last 30 years. I am quoting here one of the leaders on the table. And then, suddenly, it all came to silence. Too naive was I, thinking that if I am working towards the greater good, people will simply rally.

Well, even if I got both leaderships agreeing with me, the resistance came from the internal division of these parties. Nobody had anything against me, my work was simply collateral damages of internal fights.

I was very upset, but since I had no authority, I moved on. I learned, gained much influence and confidence. I was on the map. It is there that I met someone special, very special.

I love and respect my best friend and partner, Tranie. She is more than a confident, but the true force allowing me to heal and find back my wings. She is the logical and managing side of my success and leadership. She was in her mid-thirties and, like every woman, needed to be reminded how beautiful she truly is. For her birthday, I hired a top photographer, one covering the stars and celebrity to immortalize the beauty of my wife and best friend.

Actually, she was the one picking them, as she was following a Vietnamese pop star and her husband. They connected and I agreed to the contract. You have to know that I know nothing of the Vietnamese music and culture. I was simply willing to please my wife.

We met in the backyard on my mansion on the river. I was being open, but with no expectation nor real interest. If they could please Tranie and make her feel beautiful, I was happy. That beer we shared with them changed the course of my life.

> "Saying YES is the beginning
> of a new opportunity, always."
> **Dr. Bak Nguyen**

I was talking to the man, the photographer. His name is Tee Tran. We connected pretty quickly and I had genuine pleasure to exchange with him. We did not talk about the weather, the transit (they were from the USA) or the Vietnamese culture, but about business and success.

Very politely, he wanted to understand what business I was in and how I made my fortune. I explained that I am a cosmetic dentist and that I was looking for a way out…

It took me 15 years to accept publicly that I became a dentist solely to please my parents and family. I succeeded because I genuinely care for people and will not give up until satisfaction. That's how my arrogance suddenly turned into confidence and trust. But I am a sensitive soul and a financier at heart. I love, no, I am leverage and speed, this box was too little for me, especially after 15 years.

When Tee Tran looked at me and suggested that I should package my success and sell it to the rest of the profession before I leave. He knows many, many dentists, people who love dentistry. Most of them suffer of depression. As he looked at me, he didn't see any sign!

Very surprised with the turn of our conversation, I inquired how he knew as much. Before he answered me, he even went on to say that if I package my mindset accordingly, I could help to change the stats on the suicidal rate of my profession, a trend that haunted dentists for nearly a century now.

It is there that he revealed himself. He moved into the USA for love and reinvent himself as a photographer. He was formally the general manager, head of marketing at Telus, one of the biggest telecom company of Canada. More than being a high ranking officer, he had the merit to have led the advent of the brand from no existence into the third most recognizable name in the country within a few years...

He left everything for love. Looking at his gorgeous wife, I could understand. We had a wonderful evening connecting, him with me and Tranie with his beautiful and charming wife, Bao Han.

The photoshoot took several days. Several days in which Tranie found a new friend in Bao Han. As they were out shopping, Tee and I resumed our entrepreneurial exchanges. By the end of the weekend, he got it into my head: before I leave the profession, I should package my mindset and success to help my peers and colleagues. A week later, I started working on the matter.

It took me 2 years to understand my journey and how I successfully avoid all of the trap of the dental profession, the depression, anxiety and emotional void leading to even worst. I even push my work to research on the reason why dentists and white coats are miserable, and share my finding in **PROFESSION HEALTH**, my 5th book.

Except for Tranie, the love of my life, I packaged everything else, building a new business model for dentists. I built a lifestyle, professional conditions and opportunity that I would have bought as I was fresh out of dental school. One that will provide me with the satisfaction of living my life to the fullest while keeping my license and career as a dentist.

You see, 15 years ago, I had a shot to become a movie producer in Hollywood. It was a long shot, but I was within the few potential candidates. Don't ask me what happened... I chose my dental license instead.

My quest was one of self-fulfilment, looking for purpose, not wealth. Looking for freedom and happiness, not settling down. Even if it sounded very not compatible with my choice of building my own clinic and being a dentist, I succeeded in both arenas, personal growth and professional success. How I did it has been distilled and repackaged into the new offer to my industry: **Mdex & Co**.

Long story short, it took me 2 years to work on my plans and to find financing. I got the favor of the financial world, intrigued by my crazy ideas. They helped me with my projections, spreading the ratio as thin as the could, lended me more and more money. They bet on me, financing with millions the reforge of my industry. They did so because they saw the potential and recognize the need. Tee was right on target!

3 years later, I cut the red ribbon at the inauguration of the first complex **Mdex & Co**, one occupying 2 floors of a skyscraper in one of Montreal's prestigious downtown location. More than being the dominant player in the city, it was simply phase one, it was a pilot. A year later, we got the green light to launch a second project. For someone with nothing but his reputation and signature to give in warranty, that speaks volume.

The **Mdex & Co** model is to free the dentist of financial burdens, administrative and overhead as much as possible while leaving him/her ownership and control. I know, it sounds paradoxical, but it is possible, we did it! The idea is to be free and happy... and we worked hard enough on the business model so it also became very, very profitable for both parties.

Two years in the making, we were profitable. But the dentists did not understand the freedom, nor the happiness message. They liked it, but they signed looking at me and my financial success, not because I was happy. I was perplexed.

They suffer from depression and isolation, they are not happy to own, not happy to work for someone else, and yet, as we gave them the opportunity, all they really want is to be rich! They think that once rich, they could buy everything else!

That's the first fatal mistake: to postpone our happiness for wealth. The idea by itself will get you on your knees. Once on your knees, there is no coming back. Somehow, even with my financial success, I never accepted to kneel, since being on the profession was already bowing down more than I could accept. I was pleasing my parents, then, my patients. Never did I kneeled to money.

I am not trying to be the smartest in the room here, and bragging is the last thing I want to do. I have too much on my plate to care about bragging. I am showing my true colors and intentions. I am also showing my misfire trying to help my peers and colleagues.

> "Don't ask someone to be what one is not."
> Dr. Bak Nguyen

That I learned the hard way. Being the oldest of a family of 3, I was in charge of leading by example, with nothing more than an empty label, saying that I was born first.

> "We are what we are. We are what we choose. There is little more one can do, but so much one can choose."
> Dr. Bak Nguyen

With that in mind, I looked back at my own journey. How from a failed movie producer I became a dentist, a loved and successful one; then, an entrepreneur who became an industry's disruptor. Yup, that was how I was first introduced on the floor of the Molson School of Business, Concordia University for my first panel.

From someone who turned down, more than once, the chance and privilege to run for office to a visionary having the favor of the finance world, from a cosmetic dentist to a world record prolific author, how did I do it?

> "I reinvented myself at each turn, leaving burdens and medals behind."
> Dr. Bak Nguyen

In a nutshell, that's my recipe. So now that we are in the midst of the **GREAT PAUSE**, as all the members of our industry understand its flaws, weaknesses and profound pains, it is time to reinvent ourselves to keep our relevancy. To prevail.

I won't say that I have the solution, but if I have managed to capture your attention within 4 weeks of confinement, from your little LCD screen, it is because the flaws and weaknesses, I saw and worked towards a fix for years by now.

As I was nominated for Ernst and Young's Entrepreneur of the year, I had to defend my nomination, writing **CHANGING THE WORLD FROM A DENTAL CHAIR**. I wrote that book within a week and got it printed and delivered within 3. That proved my entrepreneurial skills and determination.

Even if I did not win the grand prize, the financial world was casting their votes for me. But in the dental world, I was still seen as a maverick and rich marginal dentist.

Before this crisis, the **GREAT PAUSE**, before we were talking about the **DENTAL DEPRESSION**, I was working on rebranding my message to please my market, the dentists. I was about to launch **THE ALPHAS**, a series of classes and seminars to get a dentist to become a millionaire. I had the track record and the knowledge to be as bold. That resonated pretty strongly, and the banks were already looking to sponsor my events. And then, **THE VIRUS** happened and we were forced into the **GREAT PAUSE**.

You know how that went. As for me, I embraced the screen to flee boredom and depression. I reached out to dentists all around the world to understand their perspectives and needs. Not all of those I wrote to responded. The Alphas did. That how I met Dr. Paul Ouellette, my friend and co-author.

That's also how I met Dr. Eric Lacoste, a community leader fighting for the children of his community more than his own survival. That's where I met Dr. Paul Dominique, a visionary thinker looking for a way to make our industry more affordable. That's how I met Dr. Robert Boyd, one of the leading heads who led the digitization of orthodontics. That's how I met Dr. and Mister Mayor Philippe Fau, from France. Suddenly, I had hope, I wasn't alone in my profession.

I have many friends, but very few are dentists. Before this pause, I couldn't stand for long a conversation amongst peer dentists, talking about surgery, gossip and possessions. And suddenly, within the time in confinement, the **ALPHAS** were coming together naturally. We all shared the same desire and core message: our world and industry are in danger and we have to rethink our old ways, very quickly!

We all knew the flaws and weaknesses of our profession, we had different opinions and alternatives to address its inefficiencies and void. And this is how we could move forward, building from our differences, not fighting to find the perfect compromise.

Forget perfection as it is a lie! Forget compromise as it will just waste time, goodwill and effort. Build from the difference! From it will emerge something even better, stronger, something with the chance to last. That, I learned from my friend and mentor, Dr. Jean De Serres.

And that's how within weeks, we, **THE ALPHAS**, captured the attention and the leadership of the dental industry. We had no invested power, but our will to share. We haven't been mandated by anyone, we are simply concerned citizen, smart ones with the gift of time.

Yesterday, we put the table to unravel Paul's plan to save the industry as it resumes with the **OUELLETTE INITIATIVE**. A few days ago, I launched with Dr. Eric Lacoste our book, **AFTERMATH**, giving to corporations and organizations a way to leverage their way out of this crisis with a win. And that's just the first 4 weeks. Next week, we will have so much more coming, bigger and bolder.

Why are we sharing as much? Because we can, because we care. Why are you listening? Because you are afraid and looking for fixes, quick fixes. That I understood as I changed my message from **FREEDOM** and **HAPPINESS** to **MILLIONAIRE**.

Well, the quick fixes, we will provide. But for those of you are seeking for more, for sustainability, for those of you who are **ALPHAS**, you will need more than a BAND-Aid. You will need to be part of the conversation to rebuild our industry, to look forward and to redefine its relevancy and role in society.

Are we teeth fixer, gums builders and holes patchers? Maybe once, but that was 100 years ago. We are so much more. Already, the teeth pulling dentist is a relic of the past. We should move on, fast!

And how shall we proceed? With a normalization, committees and protocols? Look where it led us! I am not saying that it is wrong, I am saying that it is not enough! If there is one thing we all learned from **THE VIRUS** and **THE GREAT PAUSE** is that we cannot put all the burdens over one central power, leaving so much resources and intelligence dormant.

And no, we are not looking for a fight either! We have enough fighting a virus and the recession coming, and we even have addressed the **DENTAL DEPRESSION** heading our way! For those of us feeling the need to contribute to rebuilding, don't wait for someone to ask for your help, rise up, you are an **ALPHA**.

For as long as I will remain, I promise to build from the difference, giving the floor to people of different opinions. Even if it is 100% opposite to mine, I will like to hear your opinion and ideas, for as long as you have a clear view and a line of thoughts we can follow.

For too long we have been complacent, for too long we've left our structures and policies without updates. Now, a simple update won't suffice anymore. With this **REBOOT**, we will need a firmware upgrade and maybe a change in operating system. That's start with building from the differences.

"The world has changed forever. Those who can adapt quickly and remain flexible with prosper."
Christian Trudeau

That's what he told me in his interview a few days ago. Christian Trudeau is a friend and mentor. He is also the man leading the financing rounds of **Mdex & Co**, seeking hundreds of million. M. Trudeau has been at the direction of several blue-chips in Canada, leading the pivot of technology.

To adapt quickly and to remain flexible. Can we do that? As a society? As a profession? I have my hopes and reserves. But if we all come together, we have a chance, not only for quick fixes, those will be the most popular and will buy us some time, but we will need much more, to leave perfection, standardization, and compromise aside to build from difference and to stay flexible. This is the only way for all of us to get out of this crisis without losing too much.

And yes, just like I learned, I won't be naive, asking for people to be more than they can be and choose. Some will be feeding solely on the quick fixes, good for them. We will provide more. But at the same time, others will be joining as **ALPHA** to share their perspectives and solutions. And we, and I, will be listening.

A few years back, I received the **GRAND HOMAGE LYS DIVERSITY**. Believe it or not, I have no idea of the meaning of the word diversity. To me, there are those competent and those who are not. Well, today, diversity, not of skins and cultures, but of ideas is what might save us. Now I realized why I got the award, they just gave it to me a few years earlier...

"Build from the difference."
Dr. Jean De Serres

This is how we will prevail. This is how we will all survive. This is how we will prosper, as one. This is **RELEVANCY**.

In times of crisis,
it is the bearer of continuity
of who/what/where we are

Dr. BAK NGUYEN

CHAPTER 3
"THE OUELLETTE INITIATIVE"
by Dr. PAUL OUELLETTE

EARN YOUR SMILE PAY-IT-FORWARD PROGRAM

Our family has been through other financial downturns in the past. In December of 2007, the **Great Recession** was at its beginning in Brevard County Florida. At first, it did not seem like a slow down. It gradually picked up steam and things got really bad.

The meltdown from the subprime mortgage crisis, deregulation in the financial industry and derivatives values crumbled caused the banks to stop lending. Tell me about it! I had recently signed up for a building mortgage indexed to the derivative market with monthly changing interest rates that floated with the European Libor index. I did not completely understand how this type of loan worked until the **Great Recession** hit our community.

I could not afford my large monthly payments for two of my medical buildings. When I approached my local banker to help us through the sudden real estate market crash, they could do nothing as part of my loan was sold to a foreign entity. The refinancing was not possible without an extremely large penalty. I was back in the box.

Thinking out of the box would not help us now. I had no choice other than defaulting and filing Chapter 11 to keep our doors open. Over the next year and a half, our patients count and revenues declined by 30% or more. I had to liquidate our practice profit-sharing plan to have enough cash to keep all our greatly appreciated team members employed.

In addition, our new President, bless his heart, in his second year of term one, made the decision to cut funding and eventually close the **Brevard County NASA Space Center**. He visited the Space Center when campaigning two years before and he PROMISED to always support the Space Program, that is, until he got in office.

He stated then, "We got your backs" or something like that. Don't believe the politicians! There were massive layoffs and transfers of Space Center employees to Houston or Huntsville. Other industries related to the Space Program also shuttered their businesses. Real Estate values plummeted! I had many sleepless nights worrying about my family and employees.

Not only did our family group practice experience the **Great Recession**, but Brevard County got a double whammy with the eventual shutdown of the Space Center. Those were our rocket-scientists highly educated patients and families we grew to love. Our business had to come up with something to maintain and maybe grow our once highly successful practices.

We had three locations with expensive overhead and many employees. We cut our local advertising budget and thought of ways to build our "Word-of-Mouth" advertising. We could not afford to do it any other way.

Our family has a long history of supporting our community with scholarships, free continuous education programs, school sponsorships, mouth guards for local athletes, dinners for referring doctors, donations to local charities and more. Sadly, we had to adjust our yearly community marketing budget and eliminate some of those programs. What could we do to keep our practice visible in a very competitive market?

For the previous two years, my son Dr. Jason and I participated in **SIFAT** (Servants in Faith and Technology) sponsored mission trips to Ecuador. When our mission team returned from Ecuador, we were called upon to reflect on that year's trip. I was asked what was the most significant benefit to me personally during the trip.

My answer was written on the children's faces, their faces expressed their gratitude. That was much more relevant than any words could describe. We also received many many hugs from the children and their parents. When you go on your first mission trip you will grow **"addicted"** just like me and would want to return every year!

The Ouellette family strongly believes in giving back to the community. We are all blessed with good health and have been afforded the opportunity to be professionally educated. Each year our family goes on one or more healthcare missions outside the USA.

In 2008, we traveled to the remote village Cayambe, Ecuador

to serve 395 patients. Our medical and dental team planed to return every year to serve another village near Quito, Ecuador.

My son, Dr Jason Ouellette, graduated from UOP San Francisco in June 2009. In October 2009 he joined me and the **SIFAT** mission team to return to Quito, Ecuador. That year the mission team served more than 450 patients.

After two mission trips to Ecuador, we launched the **Earn Your Smile program** to help those in this country who need financial help for orthodontic work. In addition to helping the charitable organizations obtain volunteers, the program seeks to instill a desire to volunteer in the youth. Volunteers must fill out **Smile Vouchers** and answer questions about what the experience meant to them.

The **Earn Your Smile program** helps young patients get braces even if their families have trouble affording them. Children can perform up to 100 hours of community service, pre-approved by my office. The receiving charity must sign a **Smile Voucher**, printed out by the patient that is available on the web, **www.EarnYourSmile.org**. Our way, to verify the volunteer work done.

The patient then turns in those vouchers and receives $12 of orthodontic work for every community service hour. The Dental Specialists office subtracts the volunteer credits from the patient's or parent's orthodontic bill.

Within a few months, the **Earn Your Smile program** spread like wildfire. We saw a significant increase in new families wanting to participate in the program. We were contacted by magazines, television stations and newspapers to describe the initiative. We were featured as one of the honored **Central Florida Humanitarians** at the organization's 2010 annual banquet. We did not pay for advertising. We could really not afford such expense in the economy of that time.

> "Giving has its rewards and it truly saved our practice from having to shut its doors."
> Dr. Paul Ouellette

After the Teledentistry initiative, Bak was looking for a quick fix to bring back patients in our chairs, not just his, but for all the dental profession. Within his video speech of 7 minutes, he mentioned something about treating those in need and those who were on the front line of this war against the invisible enemy.

Well, what do you know, and we never talked about the matter together. I opened up and told him about our **Earn Your Smile program**. He listened and thanked me. A few hours later, he called me back and ask for my blessing to redeploy the **Earn**

Your Smile program on an international level, renaming it **THE OUELLETTE INITIATIVE**.

I must say how flattered I was to listen to him pitching me back my own initiative. I was already ready to give, but with his contagious laugh and positive energy, Bak is someone hard to say NO to! And we agreed on the **OUELLETTE INITIATIVE** even before the first summit took place.

Imagine my surprise at the end of the first **INTERNATIONAL DENTAL SUMMIT** when Dr. Bak announced a surprise at the closing of the event. It was 2 speech videos with his eloquence. The first one was announcing the release of **AFTERMATH**, a book he has written within 2 weeks (since the beginning of **THE ALPHAS**), co-written with another **ALPHA** from Canada, Dr. Eric Lacoste, also present on the panel that day.

The closing speech video was on **THE OUELLETTE INITIATIVE**, with eloquence and patriotic music. I had tears in my eye listening to Bak's words repurposing my **Earn Your Smile program**. But now, it was not only my clinics that we were saving, but all the clinics around the world that would like to join!

A week later, we held that summit, a third initiative of **THE ALPHAS**. I took the floor and expose the why, the how and all the fine printed required to deploy such initiative.

A brother from another mother. I must say that I do not greet everyone with such affection. Before the summit, I went through **AFTERMATH**, and without influence from my part, both Bak and Eric were talking about the same principle, to join and give back, even when we were not in the best financial situation.

Bak called it, to **LEVERAGE GREED**. I found his wording very colorful, but I agree and respect its essence. He convinced me to not hold anything back. That Friday afternoon, at **THE OUELLETTE INITIATIVE** of the **INTERNATIONAL DENTAL SUMMIT**, I took the floor and gave it my all, in the **OUELLETTE**'s name, in the name of philanthropy, in the name of dentistry.

For information and downloadable **Smile Voucher** forms, visit **www.EarnYourSmile.org**. Feel free to use any copy and to modify to fit your business. Support your clients or patients with more affordable goods and services.

This strategy may be helpful to your business for a more affordable marketing budget as we come out of the CV-19 pandemic. Patients and parents will also have some skin in the game when they perform **pay it forward** services in the community. This will get everybody talking about your business or practice.

After 40-plus years of private orthodontic practice, my sons Jonathan and Jason Ouellette acquired the family dental speciality practice last year. I am doing this for them. I am doing this for the future of the profession. I am doing this because I can!

You too could survive this road bump, you can even build better and stronger from it. We did. Nothing is more exciting and scary than the uncertainty of the future. Well, this time, we've seen it before and we know how to patch the way.

THE OUELLETTE INITIATIVE is there to help you through this unprecedented crisis, one that will be called the **GREAT DENTAL DEPRESSION**.

To use Bak's word, open your heart and open your mind, we have laid out the steps to safer grounds.

This is how we will prevail. This is how we will all survive, This is how we will prosper, as one. This is **RELEVANCY**.

Dr. BAK NGUYEN

CHAPTER 4
"THE VOID"
by Dr. BAK NGUYEN

"First know who you are. Then, learn to know who the other person is, then, and only then, talk."
Dr. Bak Nguyen

You have an idea of who we are, Paul and I, and the **ALPHAS**. Now, let find out who you are. Who we are, as a whole, as a profession?

This is not my first dive in that pool. 2 years ago, I spent considerable resources and time to interview and gather information on our profession. I wanted to understand why we, health professional, white coats, as we are the forces of good of this world, are we so vulnerable to depression and worse. Especially dentists, we are amongst the highest professions at risk for depression and suicide, and that backs up to generations of dentists.

I shared my thoughts and those of who I interviewed in my 5th book, **PROFESSION HEALTH**, with many guest authors. We even had a research project co-financed with the federal government to establish a long term study on the matter, at a dental level. Too bad, the negotiation fell through with the researchers. The grants are still there, we will pick up where we left as soon as we will find the right fit. I say we, because **Mdex & Co** is bigger than myself.

Then, I moved on to other horizons. I do not wait nor fight an uphill battle for its merits or morality. I hit where I see a clear and swift victory, where I can create leverage. The leverage I created, to the minds, I extended my hand, but it is not my power nor place to change them. Until **COVID-19** happens.

I went out and reached out for people, leaders in my industry. I have to say that until that point, very little were the friends I had in my own field. We couldn't seem to connect and share a great exchange with my peers dentists. Then, I met Paul, I met Eric. With me, they were **THE ALPHAS** not fitting in.

Together, we found hope and synergy to empower one another, to support each other to make a difference. We each had our unique views and opinions. Our ideas did not compete with one another, they showed us a broader perspective of who we were, as a whole, as a profession.

You will hate reading the following, but there is no other way, before we could talk and evolve, one must know who he/she really is. Even if we might not be exactly it from at a personal level, just by following the lane of our profession, we are all exactly it. We are the following:

SELF-CENTERED

From the cradle of dental school, we had to compete for our acceptance, for our obedience to the rules and to authority. As we were greeted with wordings of **"elite"** and **"crème de la crème"**, we submitted ourselves for even more conditionings, to the rules, to perfection, to be the best, to beat the other guy standing next to us.

Too dramatic? What is our main mean to evaluate ourselves? To see how we scored from an arbitral test and compare our performance with the average! At first, we all want to be above the average, that's what got us here in the first place. Then, competing with stronger and more resilient minds, we found our peers to slowly sank into the new average.

We all did. Even the best amongst us who were leading the curve, they all went on for another curve until they too, sank into the average, another average. And then, we all looked back and saw how far we went. Looking back gave us a sense of accomplishment and pride, that's our first mistake.

For one we should never look back, all it does is to give us a false sense of reality. Those people you are looking down to, they are your bosses, your real bosses, those you shall serve! Those people you share your average with, they are not your competitors, but partners to join forces with. Can you see that our role in society was not to move up from one average to the next, but to raise the average as we become ready? That's the turn we missed, all of us.

Sure, eventually, Life will show us our place and train us into humility, but that void of vision and leadership, we got from dental school, too busy to run the **LADDERS OF CORPORATE ACADEMIA**. And then, that was replaced with the ladders of boards and certifications, in the name of the protection of the public and the quest for perfection.

> "Perfection is a lie."
> Dr. Bak Nguyen

Anyone who has done anything of worth will tell you as such. The perfection is made later in the narrative and by those following behind. The law of statistic is condemning you to fail, sooner or later! We are doctors, we do not have the right to failure, that's comprehensible, but aren't we scientists?

> "The last I checked, medicine is a science, not an art!"
> Dr. Bak Nguyen

And that's our second mistake, to misunderstand the difference between science and art.

SCIENCE VERSUS ART

The basis of science is to establish a hypothesis, to prove that hypothesis right or wrong, and to reevaluate to readjust and learn. That's how science works. Well, in our hands, it became: you make an educated guess with your diagnosis, then you proceed with your treatment plan (within your expertise and training) and if things are going well, you move on to the next patient, repeating the same pattern.

But if the outcome is not as desired, that power to reassert and re-evaluate has been given to a third party, one looking down on us as the burden of the proof lays over our shoulder. It surely feels like we are guilty until proven otherwise.

That's how the medical field is structured. I understand the need of protecting the public and agree with the logic. What is perverted is that it left a void, one we filled with more regulation and training, not means to understand and evolve on a personal level. We were back to school, day one!

"We are nothing but glorified workers."
Dr. Bak Nguyen

That's what I meant writing that quote. We are surgeons and skilled artists highly trained within on craft, but not thinkers, not scientists. That's the void of vision and leadership we are all suffering from. Those are the lies of our profession brought to the next level, one where we are conditioned to ignore that void…

More than the rat race of working for our money, since we are made stronger and selected as such, we are running in the double wheel of the rat: one of money to sustain our lives, and one of CE credits to stay within the means and the regulations. And from there, it all went to hell!

> "The best prisons are the one you polished
> with your tongue and affection."
> Dr. Bak Nguyen

Our status, our position, our wealth, they are all based on the license we hold. It is not a right, but a privilege. Bullshit! That's what those people putting themselves over our head want us to believe. It is a duty! You matter because you serve. You succeed because you care and you have because you gave. After all, people are calling you doctor, no?

Surely, we are not doctors in philosophy. People are calling us doctors because they want to trust us with their health, their money, their well-being. Even if our art is treating teeth and bone, soft tissues and grafts, above all, we are treating a person, a soul. How far are we from that?

Before you see this as an insult, please consider the last time you felt good connecting with a patient, not just proud of treating an impossible case? We are doctors, we've been trained as scientists, not just skilled workers.

And that's the dichotomy of our reality. To fill the void of re-evaluating and learning, we have a tribunal of "peers" looking down on us. That's alright given the importance of our task, but with what have we filled the void? The spiritual void of vision, leadership and evolution since dental school?

Look at the pyramid of Maslow and you will clearly see the glass ceiling over your head, at the 2/3 of the pyramid. As the lower layers of the pyramid are about survival and reproduction, the middle ones are about differentiation (beating the average and the guy sitting next to us).

But then, we are aspiring for more, for purpose and self-fulfilment, which can never happen if we keep running the lanes of competition to climb the ladders of corporate academia, of corporate licensing. That's our glass ceiling.

COVID-19 shattered the illusion and showed us the true choices we made and accepted by default. That void of human connectivity, of self-evolution, of purpose, it does not go away. Like any pain, it lays dormant and ignored until it has hardened and taken root. And them, just like a cancer of the soul, it will spread its poison of resentment. The day you'll lose contact with love and hope, that day, the **VOID** will swallow you in a single bite.

What's wrong with being an artist? Well, those who succeed are feeding on the praises and excesses to keep their passion growing. What are you feeding yourself with? Your fees, your CE credits, your dusty diplomas and your debts?

I am not judging, I am one trapped soul too. But how do I know so much? Because I was there looking at us. Bored in seminars and classroom, I started looking around to see how my peers were doing. I saw and took note. Then, I suffered the symptoms myself, at the beginning of my career. I was depressed, sure, but I was too young to end my life.

I found purpose, not in my art, but in the people who put their trust in me. I was thirsty for genuine connections. Their trust pushed me to perfect my skills and craft to deliver them, not perfection, but harmony and satisfaction. That's how I slowly grew apart from the friendship of my peers to develop friendship and genuine connections with those I treat, because we shared something genuine, not comparing our craft.

> "I succeeded as a dentist because my patients gave me purpose and the need to perfect my skills and craft."
> Dr. Bak Nguyen

Why am I talking about myself here? Because it is easier for you to judge me than to judge yourself. But soon enough, you can relate to my pain and my logic. Soon enough, you can see the path and the patterns, unless you choose to ignore them once again.

THE LIE OF PERFECTION

That's the *kryptonite* pinning all of us down. It was intended to keep us humble. Added to our habits of comparing ourselves with the average, it became an obsession and it tunneled vision us on a quest without significance.

More than once, I read on walls of social media, who amongst us, dentists, have made history? Who has risen outside of the corporate ladders of our industry… a small industry overlooked by all at the light of **COVID-19**? Have we really spent much of our lives building such irrelevancy?

Waiting in the **GREAT PAUSE** and put aside, the only smart thing to do was to bank our CE credits to make the most of out the situation and to refrain ourselves to look down in the abyss ahead. Well, I got with the **ALPHAS** and brought solutions on the table. The first question, even within our ranks, was: it is perfect?

> "To counterbalance your urge for perfection,
> look at the alternatives."
> Dr. Bak Nguyen

The reason why I am saying that **COVID-19** has made the light on our glass ceiling is that now, we do are do die. And we do not have much time to debate or to look for perfection. All we are looking at is the best possible outcome, looking at the alternatives within reach.

We did that. We are doing that. We are pushing the alternatives. If we aren't, we will leave the **VOID** be filled by someone else's ambition with motivation and views we may not share. But how to talk when we do even know what we are inside? Isn't this a familiar feeling?

In my previous chapter, I talk about quick fixes. Well, I can tell you that taking the lead with the **ALPHAS** to find solutions to the crisis of our profession, I saw the trends and collective behaviors, people (doctors and professors) are looking for band-aid and debating for the perfect tools. I can tell you that in parallel, they missed out on the chance to go beyond the glass ceiling.

All because they were too occupied, either by fear of the abyss or by their own habits of looking for the perfect solution. I say they, because this time, I was on the other side, looking for the true cause of our irrelevancy and why, not only were we subjected to depression and suicidal tendency, but why we were put so easily aside, we, the elite, we the doctors.

The Tsunami is coming and this is merely the first wave. The bigger one is coming, the recession. But to us, white coats, it will not be a recession, it will be a **DENTAL DEPRESSION**, one flooding everything and those trapped under the glass ceiling might not make it. Do you now see the picture?

Within this journey, I met with many people, different people, doctors. Most were authentic and genuine, generous with their time and knowledge, animated with the desire to share and to grow. Well, we are not above the law of numbers… and we also met some lesser minds… I will only share this quote that I consider as a fact:

> "One cannot be a thought leader with a small heart…"
> Dr. Bak Nguyen

Forget your trivial quest for perfection, if you've spent 10, 20 even 30 years looking for it, you must know that it does not exist. Look beyond your art and craft and remind yourself why people are calling you doctor. Don't look back and don't look down, your hopes are up. So look up with an open mind and yes, you will have to open your heart too!

Only with an open heart, will you find the purpose to push yourself ahead and to finally break the glass ceiling! This time, time isn't on your side. So do it, and do it quickly. If you are about to break the glass ceiling, why are you still afraid of breaking some eggs of pride and lies?

See the **VOID** and start filling it. This time, you won't be able to blindside it, not anymore.

This is how we will prevail. This is how we will all survive. This is how we will prosper, as one. This is **RELEVANCY**.

Dr. BAK NGUYEN

CHAPTER 5
"THE HAPPINESS FORMULA"
by Dr. ANIL GUPTA

My name is Anil Gupta. I had the pleasure of bumping into Dr. Bak by accident. Well, was it an accident? Actually, it was no accident. Everything that we do as human beings is related to our vibrational energy. I could see a great beautiful energy around Dr. Bak. I was immediately drawn to him and his energy, and vice versa.

Within seconds we knew that we were on the same wavelength and we had the same values and virtues. We both wanted to make a difference. So we started talking, and in an instant we had struck up a fabulous rapport.

When you are in this zone, amazing things can happen very rapidly. We even did an interview, there and then. This is spontaneity. This is seeing what there is to see and taking action.

"Life is not about us but the difference that we make."
Dr. Anil Gupta

There comes a point in your life when you realize the **secret to living is giving**. In these difficult times, we need to get some clarity around our own happiness levels. We often make things appear worse than they really are.

It can create a lot of fear and confusion. We need clarity. Our success depends upon our actions and inactions. What could you do to make your chances of success much higher? What new skills could you learn? One sentence changed my life.

"Be so amazing that you cannot be ignored, and if you are ignored, it does not matter as you will have become a totally different and successful person."
Dr. Anil Gupta

There is actually a beautiful, powerful formula for happiness that can bring focus to the area of our life that we need to focus on the most with the biggest impact. It works!

$$H = G \times G \times G$$
Happiness = Give x Grow x Gratitude

The First G

The first thing you have to do is to **Give**. You have to give your time, love, energy, joy, commitment, money, gift, presence etc. WITHOUT wanting anything in return. It has to be a pure gift with a pure intention. It is all about the intent. In the moment you give authentically the pain and suffering will disappear.

> Perform 10 acts of kindness in the next two days.
> Notice how it makes you feel.
> Make sure you don't wish for anything in return.
> Write down how this makes you feel.

The Second G

You have to **Grow** Emotionally, Physically, Spiritually and Mentally. Have a look at your life and see which one of these you need to work on. Be brutally honest. What do you spend your time thinking about most of the time? Is it your emotions, your health, your spiritual side or your mental aptitude? There is no better time than now to quieten the mind and to grow your life. You will reap the benefits for the rest of your life. Health and relationships are the cornerstones of a happier and fulfilled life.

> Keep a diary of your positive and negative thoughts.
> Do something to improve your physical health.
> Do something mentally challenging.
> Read a self-development book.

The Third G

You have to be **Grateful**. Be grateful for what you have and do not focus on what you do not have.

Write down **50 things you are grateful for**. This may sound a lot. It is like a muscle, the more you use, it the easier it gets. Things to be grateful for could be your friends, family, clothing, roof over your head, health, wealth, transportation, phone, internet, shoes, teeth, feet, skin, air, sunshine etc.

Write down **20 things you have accomplished** in your life (being born, walking, talking etc.) As you write these down, please notice how it makes you feel. It will lift you up!

Now the beautiful thing about this formula is that **IT ALWAYS WORKS!**

Whenever you feel that you are not as happy, perhaps you could look at the **Happiness Formula**. Work on the lowest G. You will see immediate results.

This is my gift to you, one for your happiness, for the happiness of those you touch, for your relevancy, as a person and, for Dr. Bak's pleasure, for the relevancy of your profession.

This is how we will prevail. This is how we will all survive. This is how we will prosper, as one. This is **RELEVANCY**.

In times of crisis,
It is the safest opportunity
to reinvent who we are.

Dr. BAK NGUYEN

CHAPTER 6
"ON THE OTHER SIDE"
by Dr. BAK NGUYEN

This book is written as I head up to my 7th week in confinement and my 5th week standing as an **ALPHA**, one for our profession. In the last 30 months, I have written many, many books. While a few were about the dental field, **PROFESSION HEALTH** is looking at why are we miserable even if we do good on a daily basis.

HOW TO NOT FAIL AS A DENTIST is mentorship to all the newcomers in our profession. Basically, I am telling how I succeed rising in a profession I despited, loved by my patients and respected by my peers. **SUCCESS IS A CHOICE** is my latest book for dentists, showing the path to become millionaires.

I was talking about happiness in the first volume, it sounded cool on stage, but people weren't as interested. Then, I talked about success, that one, people reacted more and were willing to buy. I was simply not ready to commit to coach and mentor doctors just yet.

I soon realized that reading isn't enough to implement change. With the third opus, I removed my white gloves and went straight to the point: talking about wealth. That, people reacted very favorable to. I realized that looking at my track record building a new dental economic model for the future of our industry.

I told you that before **COVID-19**, the **ALPHA** brand was built to launch masterclass, seminars and boardroom coaching masterminds to train dentists to become millionaires, using their skills and leveraging on the tools we provide, Mdex's tool.

Then, in the midst of **THE PAUSE**, I met with Paul and a few hours later, Eric. And so started a conversation, a genuine one. Eric was astonished by my ability to push forward and to rally the attention. He was looking at what I was doing and wondered if there wasn't a place to build not leaving our weakest links behind.

He was right, I went on to collaborate with him to write **AFTERMATH**, business after **THE GREAT PAUSE**. That book is not intended for the dental industry, but to all the C-class, the corporate decision-makers.

My part within **AFTERMATH** was to find a way to leverage ourselves (as corporations and a society) out of this crisis ahead, with a win. It is by far, my best work for the future of our society, not lecturing about what to do, but showing a way out, built from the best skillset of the C-class: **GREED** and **LEVERAGE**.

I am not judging, I am one of them! The only difference is that this time, I am sharing my blueprint and war maps. We wrote this book within 2 weeks. By the 14th day, Apple Books was releasing it in 51 countries. By the 3rd week, Amazon approved it for print on demand. In itself, this was a highlight in my career and a new world record.

Even if we addressed the business world, we learned from the dental world to formulate our plans and remedies. The dental world was the first to whom we launched our message, to build better and with more leverage. I have to tell you that we were surprised by the lack of interest. It killed our morale for the rest of that week, Eric and I.

But aren't we **ALPHAS**? Paul Ouellette came as reinforcement to finish the summits of that week with a victory, delivering **THE OUELLETTE INITIATIVE**, a quick fix that could get most of the dental clinics around the world back in business as soon as the confinement is lifted and, at the same time, addressed our PR image. People loved the fix, they did not care much about the PR nor philanthropy.

Didn't I tell you that from the beginning of this crisis I was fighting alongside with the local leaders of our profession to have some recognition from the governments for our staff and ourselves, and to have the insurances companies to honor the policies they sold us. I was the person holding the phone, literally between the minister and the leaders.

I had the minister's ear since we were friends, but then, an article about how dentists were suffering during this crisis came out on the newspaper. Even if that article was straight and fair, making the light on how the dentists were left with nothing, the population plagued it with a storm of bad comments, in the biggest midst of solidarity! That took away all the leverage we had and our voice as a profession. It was radio silence after that, from all my contacts in power...

I don't blame them, I would have done the same thing in their position. But that showed me clearly how deep was our problem, one much broader than our internal isolation and depression, it was one of relevancy.

In short, even if we are respected, even loved by those under our care, those who could not afford our care (the rest of the population) hated us!

That answered my first question, why are we depressed even if we are the forces of good! Because our relevancy is limited and our habits of competing amongst ourselves sealed the glass ceiling at the 2/3 of **Maslow's Pyramid**.

All of that was before I started writing **AFTERMATH**. The release of **AFTERMATH** to the dental world showed me our limitations. As **AFTERMATH** was basically building from the class ceiling up, we lost most of our peers and members... except for the **ALPHAS** who started joining from different corners of the world.

What is my point? My point is that the **ALPHAS** will make it out, I will make it out, somehow. What about all of those beneath the glass ceiling? As Paul came with a solution to open a safe passage, they will still have to open their heart to pass through that bridge. I just do not get it! Are we all smart people, the best top 10% back in school? What are the alternatives, really?!

To line up asking for help from our governments and officials when we clearly do not have the support of the public? To fight an uphill legal battle with the insurance companies that have the means to spread the legal procedures long enough to have us buried twice before the first audience? Or to head back in our old ways, spending in marketing to fight for patients?

None of those will get us out of the water before the bottom of the pyramid is entirely flooded. If anything, it might keep us busy before we are all swept away by the second wave of the Tsunami, the **DENTAL DEPRESSION**.

I am no prophet, so you don't have to throw rocks at me. I am one within our ranks, one that stood silence for much too long. And now that I clearly see what's coming, I am building that bridge through the glass ceiling, one that will provide safe passage, but again, I can't force you to listen. I can only invite and inspire you to do so.

"The harder one works, the luckier one gets."

That happened right between the launch of **AFTERMATH** and the **OUELLETTE INITIATIVE**. Other **ALPHAS** from our field started to join our initiatives. Some are titans our their field, some are visionary thinkers, some others had done it before, now they are sharing their secrets.

That table was surely unusual since **ALPHAS** do not play well with one another. Well, the times have changed and the age of competition is over. If we do not collaborate and share, we will all disappear. The **ALPHAS** understood that.

As they were joining, they replenished my hope and determination to keep fighting for all, not just saving myself and bearing regrets looking back later on.

We must build our new foundations from the glass ceiling and up. The only way through is from sharing. Yes, sharing. That's how the **ALPHAS** got through, even if we spent most of our lives learning and training to fight, the day we left that aside, we rose, almost effortlessly with the blessing of mother nature!

And how did we build bigger, bolder and stronger? Because we never lost contact with our base, we know who we are serving: the population, and now, you!

RELEVANCY is aiming to raise all of us to life and business post-**COVID-19**. Just like the most corporations, we will have to rebuild our industry from the ground up. It's not even a choice, it is: do or die. Dentists in France used to believe that no matter what will happen, our profession was safe. Well, not anymore! And that's coming from a country who elected dentists for mayors, more than once!

With Paul, we are not aiming to rectify the flaws and remedy the void, even if Paul is kind and generous in nature, he will be patching your wounds with kindness and quick fixes to keep you alive along the way. My job is to build in record time that bridge to safe passage, one through the glass ceiling and to show you how to walk through it, all of you.

I have also invited the **ALPHAS** to join in with their own perspectives. Even if most of them will be writing their own books, they all agreed to join in for a chapter in **RELEVANCY**. Dr. Paul Dominique, Dr. Eric Lacoste, Dr. Anil Gupta Dr. Nach Daniel have already confirmed their presence in **RELEVANCY**.

Paul has a dynasty of dentists in his family. I am sure that he too, will have other **ALPHAS** to sign up. This isn't about opinions, it is about solutions. Since no one has ever encountered such crisis, there is no perfection, no proven nor better way. It is to be above the glass ceiling or to stay under. That will be a choice each of us has to make.

Today, I have a great friend and international speaker joining our summit: Dr. Anil Gupta. He is in a quest to impact a billion lives, spreading happiness. His recipe of happiness is the 3G: Give, Gratitude and Grow. He stands with people like Sir Richard Branson, Anthony Robbins and has coached Mike Tyson. Within the next few months, he has an event with the Dalai Lama planed…

Well, I abused my friendship and asked Dr. Gupta for a talk to our public. He gladly accepted, saying that he can't say NO, especially to someone as positive as me. But then, he had to adjust his message. We came up with: **FIGHTING DEPRESSION**. That, our ranks and our peers will understand!

How did we change from the formula of happiness to fighting depression? Can you see how deep are our wounds and corrupted our source code?

> "Wording isn't the surface, but the path to a much, much deeper truth, our of identity."
> Dr. Bak Nguyen

On the 64 books I've written, only 3 are about dentistry. This is the 4th. Most of the others are about philosophy and our quest of identity, our personal quest. My famous quote is: "Our legend can only begin the day that we are out of quest of identity."

Well, that quest I know. Even if my goal here is to build a bridge for you to cross before the arrival of the **DENTAL DEPRESSION**, I will fast track your quest of identity. That will also mean that I will have to help our profession to find its identity and purpose beyond teeth.

> "I treat people, not teeth."
> Dr. Bak Nguyen

This is how I made my career as a dentist. This is how I've beaten the odds of depression and success, despite that I wasn't at my place in a dental chair. That's also how I found allies and friends to support me to build the new dental economic model. Of course, I will talk about **Mdex & Co** and what it stands for, but this is only once we are on the other side of the glass.

I started with building for financial freedom and happiness. To make it sustainable, I added recipes of success, almost foolproof, but it wasn't enough. To make it appealing, I added wealth to it, not taking away anything else from the deal. That will make my fortune, but it won't be enough to safe all of you, to save our profession. Writing **AFTERMATH**, I added another dimension, relevancy and social impact. That's how we won't be left behind.

The direct application is the **OUELLETTE INITIATIVE**. Do that and you will have crossed the bridge to safer grounds. It is still just the beginning of your journey. Now, we need to rebuild.

AFTERMATH will explain to you the blueprints and inspiration to not escape the war, but to win it.

It will be for each of you to find your own purpose and your way through this. As a profession, we are the sum of all its individuals. No one can dictate how we will stand and be, how relevant we will be, but each of us summing up. No board, no school, no authority can do that, it is for us to find the will to finally fill up our **VOID** of vision and leadership.

I won't dare say that I will fill it. I will just share with you how I filled up mine. Paul is doing the same thing, but with a much gentler touch. Our peers **ALPHAS** will each do that from their unique perspective. We will share with you. We hope to inspire you, but it will be up to you to decide. Nonetheless, we will be there, helping you to get to the other side.

> "From our difference, we will build better, bolder, stronger."
> Dr. Jean De Serres

This is how we will prevail. This is how we will all survive, This is how we will prosper, as one. This is **RELEVANCY**.

In times of crisis,
It is the perfect opportunity
To re-invent who we are.

Dr. BAK NGUYEN

CHAPTER 7
"THE JOY OF GIVING"
by Dr. PAUL OUELLETTE

My family and I have been very blessed. At age 28 years, the second year out of my orthodontic program, I met a beautiful woman Patricia. She was an orthodontic patient that was referred to my very first orthodontic office in a suburb of Atlanta called Austell, Georgia.

The year was 1973. Patricia was referred to my practice by two of my Oral Maxillofacial Facial Surgeon colleagues, Drs. Louis Belinfante and Richard Jackson. My future wife was a surgical nurse that often worked with Drs. Belinfante and Jackson. She was very skilled at what she did and was one of the top LPNs at Cobb General and Smyrna Hospitals.

I remember attending an orthognathic surgery for one of my orthodontic patients. Patricia came to the surgery with me that day to observe. Dr. Belinfante had hired a new surgical assistant that was having trouble passing the correct instruments and setting up his surgical handpiece. Frustrated, he asked Patricia to scrub in and help the new girl. It was like night and day seeing Patricia take over.

Watching her work with Dr Belinfante was like watching a professional musician playing a classical masterpiece. She knew every surgical instrument and anticipated when he needs them. He did not raise his head once to ask for an instrument during the whole procedure.

She was also very polite and treated the new assistant with respect and kindness. I could see her fine qualities as an assistant and my future wife that day. When it was time for me to help Dr. Belinfante with ortho-surgical fixation, I scrubbed in and re-entered the room.

I quickly contaminated the surgical field as a newbie that was not completely familiar with OR protocols. Thank God, Patricia came at the rescue! She helped me re-glove and guided me through OR surgical protocols.

She later became one of my orthodontic assistants and office manager, aka Boss, for more than 25. My sister in law, Jeannette, was my first orthodontic assistant. She worked with me for more than 40 years. Jeannette now lives with us, spending time with her grandchildren in Atlanta and helping us raise ours in Florida. When I come home every night, I come through the front door I say: "Honeys, I'm home!"

Not only was Patricia smart, talented and a kind person, but she was also absolutely drop-dead gorgeous, inside and out. I tell my sons you are only allowed to marry one time so make sure to pick the right person. It will save you a ton of money and heartaches.

My sons have followed my lead. One married a tax attorney & accountant and the other a veterinarian. We have 5 new grandbabies to help raise.

From the above description of my future bride, one can see why I violated one of the first rules of being a young orthodontist in his first practice. DO NOT date your patients! I broke that rule immediately. I often tell my friends that Patricia paid her orthodontic bill in full over the two years I treated her and now I get to pay all her bills for life! No complaints!

We are going on year 45 of our life's journey together. As long as I agree with Pat's wishes things run smoothly. She often tells me: "Everyone is entitled to Pat's opinion!" I totally agree! Sadly for me, she is usually always right in her judgment of people and doing the right thing. She passed this trait to our children.

My wife blessed me with two sons, Dr. Jonathan and Dr. Jason. We also had a daughter Danielle that was on track to become the family's Oral Surgeon. After 4 years of pre-dental studies and several summers observing oral and periodontal surgeries at my son Jonathan's dental school in Bogota Colombia, she decided to pursue advertising and marketing. She is now an art director at an agency in NYC.

Patricia bought her 6-year-old daughter Cindy to our marriage and we raised her together. We had a recent family tragedy two years ago when we lost our then 50-year-old Cindy. We will never get over our loss, but we will enjoy our future happy times with Cindy always in our minds.

Looking back 50 years of my professional and family experiences the secret to our success was ALWAYS treat each other as you would want to be treated yourself.

> "Be a giver, not a taker! Always stay motivated
> and offer to help each other."
>
> Dr. Paul Ouellette

Apply this simple life's rule to all friends, family members and new acquaintances. We also observed my mother Lanette living her life to the fullest and guiding us. She taught us by example. She is a role model for our family.

When my brother Mike and I were growing up, my mother was divorced and a single mother the first 8 years of our lives. Lanette, now 96, was a concert cellist that played in the Winter months every year for the Miami Symphony.

My mother's parents helped raised us with Lanette for many years. My grandfather was a Pharmacist that owned a drug store on the Ocean City New Jersey Boardwalk that was open for the summer season only. My grandmother was in charge of the drug store soda and food counter.

I remember her sandwiches with the crust always cut off on all sides. It's still hard to eat the crust when I have a sandwich. She spoiled us early in our lives. We all learned early the **Joy of Giving** from our family by example.

It is definitely better to give than to receive as it makes you feel better than the recipient of the gift or kind gesture. I could not scientifically find a reason why we all were so happy when giving, serving our patients and communities.

I did some online research and came across a 2007 article on the **NIH-National Institutes of Health**, Research Matters website. The article was saying there may be a biological basis for **pleasure centers** in the brain becoming hyper-activated from charitable activities.

This happens when people decide to give away money to charity rather than keeping it all for themselves. This also may be a reason why some people contribute to the public good, even at a personal cost!

In the article, they cited a research project at the University of Oregon. They used an imaging technique known as functional magnetic resonance imaging or fMRI. The technique looked at areas of the brain that are activated by acts of kindness and giving.

The study was supported by the National Institute on aging or NIA and the National Science Foundation. I am starting to get up there in years. You could say, I am an expert in aging! Maybe if I continue to emphasize our families' **joy of giving**, I will continue to be a "young" out of the box thinker. There may be hope to stay young like our Mother well into the 80s and 90s.

The study was published in the June 15, 2007 issue of Science Magazine. Brain scans showed different results. Receiving money, seeing money going to a good cause or donating money, all activated similar pleasure-related centers deep in the brain.

There may be scientific evidence for our Joy of Giving. When a member of the Ouellette Family wakes up every morning we try to feel great and look at the positive, never dwell on the negative. One exception, DO NOT talk to Patricia until she has her first cup of coffee!

Let us look at some positive effects of donating money and services to charity. I did some additional online research to find out why the Ouellettes mostly have positive attitudes and experience that feel-good happiness when helping others.

I came across a blog by Jay Robinson. In his blog, the author references the 2014 **Atlas of Giving**. In the year 2014, US-based giving decreased by 3.2%. There were a variety of reasons for that decrease. At that time, there were rising interest rates, a possible stock market correction and employment compensation was decreasing.

We are experiencing similar conditions now due to the CV-19 pandemic. Maybe there will be another financial recession or depression. This will not be a good reason for one to not continue philanthropic charitable giving.

> "In the coming financial recession or maybe depression, I DO NOT want to be DEPRESSED, as well."
> Dr. Paul Ouellette

We will continue to do our part to make this a better world for our family and others. This will be our **recession ANTIDOTE**!

Robinson described the **9 positive effects of donating** money to charity.

1. Experience more pleasure

Most of us experience more pleasure within themselves when they give money or help another person that may be depressed or feeling helpless. It takes a Village is an old adage. In the coming financial downturn, we all need to work together to prevent world poverty. In the end, you will get more pleasure out of your acts of kindness than the receiver.

2. Help others in need

We all know or will know people in need. It may be a young doctor working as an associate that had to be furloughed or terminated. It could be one of our team members with young children being home-schooled. The point is, find ways to help them until the schools are clear to open again after the pandemic.

3. Tax Deduction

In most cases, charitable giving of money is tax-deductible. There is information on the IRS website that shows approved charities. Keep track of your cash donations as you will need receipts for taking the deductions.

4. Bring more meaning to your life

I like the **Bring More Meaning to Your Life** positive effect. Our family is very thankful for our financial success. Most of it was possible because we had a positive caring attitude 24/7.

> "Returns on an Act of Kindness can be many fold including words of your deeds spreading like a wildfire."
> Dr. Paul Ouellette

Our pay it forward **EarnYourSmile program** helped us out of a deep financial hole by acquiring more patients as the word spread. New patients referred other family members, neighbors and fellow workers. It will work again for the families in the current economy.

5. Promote generosity in your Children

Children learn from example, not words. When your children and employees see how happy you are when giving, it makes a positive impact on them for life. As our children finished school and started their own practices, it was obvious that they were brought up to serve their patients with compassion and never focus solely on profits.

Both my sons have many more positive social media reviews that most competing practices in their communities. It does not cost money to earn great reviews and endorsements.

6. Motivate friends and family

Be kind to your team members and set an example of the positive caring attitude in your practice. You will be able to recruit like-minded employees as we did. That was one of our main **secrets for our success**. Hire caring givers, not selfish entitled takers!

> "Do not tolerate miserable people if they can not be rehabilitated and become givers."
> Dr. Paul Ouellette

7. Realize that every little bit helps

Every little bit helps to make a difference. Many acts of charity can be small things such as giving a few dollars to a patient that followed your home care instructions or the little brother or sister that came to the office with the patient.

My favorite thing to do when a 4 or 5-year-old comes with their big brother or sister to an orthodontic appointment is to have them assist us in the operatory. We give them oversized gloves and a face mask. At the conclusion of the appointment, I would give each child $1 or $2 to go to McDonald's to get some ice cream.

Deadly pathogens and everyone's safety will not make this act of kindness, possible post-pandemic. I will miss the look in their eyes when they became part of the dental visit and were duly compensated. We will find other ways.

8. Improve personal money management

Establishing a monthly dollar amount to donate to community charities will also help you be a better money manager in general. You will learn how to set budgets so you can continue to pay your expenses and have money available for giving you that dose of self-satisfaction we all need.

> "Giving is a treatment for stress."
> Dr. Paul Ouellette

It has helped our family in financial bad times and won us recognition as givers in our community.

9. Volunteer, if you can't give

If you do not have extra cash to donate we recommend you volunteer your time. There are many local organizations such as Goodwill, Habitat for Humanity, Schools, Police Departments, Hospitals, Day Care Centers and more than will gladly welcome your time. You will also experience the **Joy of Giving**, recognition from the receiving organization and build a great reputation in the community.

Going forward, we all have our flaws and misery. Well, try **GIVING** as a remedy. I can assure you, you will be better off and ahead, every single time!

This is how we will prevail. This is how we will all survive. This is how we will prosper, as one. This is **RELEVANCY**.

Dr. BAK NGUYEN

CHAPTER 8
"HUMILITY, FLEXIBILITY AND ADAPTABILITY"
by Dr. BAK NGUYEN

A few days ago, I had the chance to sit down with my friend and mentor, Christian Trudeau, through a zoom teleconference, of course, adapting to the new reality of **COVID-19**. Well, he accepted to be interviewed and recorded so our conversation will be useful to many.

M. Trudeau led the digitalization and automation of the Montreal Stock Exchange and many other Stocks Exchange in the world in the 80s. At the forefront of technology, he then went on to found and lead, as CEO/founder, the e-commerce division of **Bell Canada**, BCE Emergis.

Within a few years, **BCE Emergis** was one of the 3 major players in e-commerce in North America. This was when we were still talking about TCP/IP, the was no internet yet.

More than once, M. Trudeau led the evolution of the **INFORMATION AGE**. Today, I wish to learn from his experience and wisdom to see through the **COVID-19** crisis, to resume better out of the **GREAT PAUSE**, to avoid the **DENTAL DEPRESSION** ahead.

Very humble, he shared with me for about half an hour. We were talking about technology and society. He kept repeating that he does not have a crystal ball to know what's ahead, but he is sure that the world has changed forever!

Looking forward, his recommendation for the leaders and entrepreneurial class is to stay humble, flexible and to adapt quickly. That's how he led the evolution from analogue to digital. Back then, there was still resistance to face, resistance to change. Today, resistance is futile… it is do or disappear. But how quickly can one readjust and readjust again and again. This was what he meant by being humble, flexible and swift.

> "Be humble, flexible and react swiftly."
> Christian Trudeau

In the world of information and technology, that made a lot of sense. The medical world is another world, one with different standards. Does this still stand? Are we so different and obeying to a different law of gravity?

People used to think that the world will always need dentists, no matter what. Well, within this crisis, dentists all around the world have been put aside with barely 3% of relevancy (emergencies to address). This speaks volume about our relevancy in society.

As most of us are connected, with a smartphone and social media, can we really stand above technology and its trends, with our ethic, boards and CE policies? That worked in the previous era, the industrialization era, but at the information age, it is still the way to structure ourselves, as a profession?

The **COVID** crisis shed light on what it means to be proactive, not just reactive. Our authorities are doing their best to win the war against an invisible enemy, and we are waiting in line behind. Was this the best distribution of resources? Of intelligence?

Better spread throughout the grid than hospitals, our network of dental clinics could have done so much to help, and yet, because we were too busy at mining our own business and fighting amongst ourselves, our relevancy was next to nothing… 3%. This is not me speaking, but the bitter reality in which we woke up every morning in confinement, on **PAUSE**.

How many amongst us have raised their voices to help and to participate in the war effort? Well, we weren't valued in the war effort, not because of discrimination, but simply because we never learned to play as team players. That **VOID** that we bear inside, everyone is smelling it!

It will take much more time and resources to address that **VOID** of vision and leadership. But today, the light has been made and you are blind if you can't see the diagnostic and its prognostic, keeping our old ways.

"To be flexible and to adapt again and again…"
Dr. Bak Nguyen

This can't come solely from a board looking for the perfect and standardized protocol nor from a University pushing for scientific proofs beyond doubts. We need more flexibility and more speed of reaction. A central command would get us through this crisis, but not a second time.

Although I am very grateful to the tremendous work of our leaders and governments to address this war, we weren't prepared and too many resources were left aside. Does it make sense to pause 90% of the workforce and applying much needed and depleted resources to feed and take care of that same workforce put on pause?

No, no blame here, no one saw what was to come, no one was prepared. But we won't have that excuse a second time! And this is an analyze as a society. What about our profession? If today you are reading this, it is because you know the risks of extinction of our kind. Not of dentists, but dentistry as we know it.

No one can oppose progress nor the forced and prompt firmware upgrade. The only question is who will make it and who will be left behind? And in every evolution, there is a normal curve of distribution... but not this one. The glass ceiling could trap the main body of our curve if we do not act fast, with humility and swiftness, again and again.

The quick fix is **THE OUELLETTE INITIATIVE**, bringing back patients in our chairs quickly while we are sending a "voluntary" workforce back to help the philanthropic organizations on the ground. But then, we will need a reflection as a profession to define our role and place in society, one beyond the teeth.

And beyond the teeth, the CE credits mainly focused on the improvement of our surgical skills, beyond the regulation of protocols of the state and provincial boards. We now need to take our place in the population and its evolution proactively, not just reacting and to fill the holes.

So how can we democratize our profession and adapt it with flexibility, swiftness and relevancy in mind? By forgetting those notions of perfection. That would be the first lie to let go.

That's humility in itself. As we are accepting that our protocols and sciences aren't perfect, we are also accepting that we are not perfect. We never were, we just drank the Kool-Aid and act as if.

Now aware of our imperfections, the chances for improvement are on the frontline of our thoughts, on a daily basis. Before, we were trained to repeat the same act over and over again with predictability. That's the art, that's step one. Beyond, is what we have to build now, a way to evolve and adapt to the evolution of society, of the planet, of our species. That's relevancy.

> "To build from the differences."
> **Dr. Jean De Serres**

If you want anything to last, to build from the differences is also the way to incorporate the workforce and impact of everyone, as one. Today, we stand united in the fight against **COVID-19**, what about tomorrow? What will be, a year from now? History taught us that sooner or later, we will fall back into complacency if our survival is not at stake anymore.

To find our relevancy is a dialogue we will need to have as a profession, amongst peers. To be humble will only happen the day we cease to drink the lies of perfection and fear. To be flexible will required a reforging of our governing system, one not balanced by an opposition, but one building from the differences.

4 years is a long time in power. It is also a time long enough to feel the entitlement of power. And that only at the top of our system, most of the institutions underneath are nominated and obey to a central directive. The counterbalance of power is the voice of the opposition and the voice of the press, talking for the people... 'when they resist the sensationalism. No one is perfect, and that's ok. Let stop pretending to be.

With this, our opposition system isn't working either, since we are condemned to do and undo as the political wind changes. Can we learn from this crisis a better way?

In the Antiquity, the Romans had a republic with 2 pro-consults, relaying power. Imagine having a system like it where 2 leaders will have to govern, alternating every year over a period of 4 years. Just like the USA system, the president and vice-president are running together, but what if the vice-president is not waiting in the line of succession, but serve as a co-president, alternating with the president instead?

Now, imagine if the 2 men are not even from the same political affiliation. Not sharing the same point of view, but still sharing the same liability, accountable for their alternate terms in power. What kind of leadership will we have? It won't be a battle for ideas and provocation anymore, since nothing is perfect, it will be a dialogue to keep things moving forward, as smoothly as possible!

The time for a clear winner and a clear loser is over. The time of half measure is also over. Now is the time to come together, to build from our difference if we want a chance to include the majority of the population and not to do and undo right after.

At the administrative level, the same structure of co-presidencies could be installed, once again, forcing flexibility, humility and swift adaptability closer to the evolution on the ground, not just ideas and quest of the perfect solution.

To the saying, if it ain't broken, don't fix it. Well, our system cannot withstand another crisis of this magnitude. Broken is not even the word. We need more than a fix, more than an upgrade, we need to redefine our relevancy and our ways, as individuals, as citizens, as a society, as a profession.

The **VOID** of vision and leadership is one of our profession. It might also be one of a greater degree of our kind, humankind. Global warming, world hunger, the failure of the capitalist system, the establishment and the injustices, our planet was working and was imperfect.

Now it has rebooted, some systems will be up and running as before and some will need much work to run, even at a fraction of its previous efficiency. Will it make sense to double down and to reinvest in a flawed and broken system or will it make more sense to upgrade it to one that could withstand the next crisis?

Please do not misinterpret my words, I am not promoting anarchy nor a revolution of any kind. I am suggesting an open dialogue to rebuild better and wiser. This might be the only good the **COVID** crisis will have brought us: to come together and to stop fighting amongst ourselves.

> "For the first time within our lifetime,
> all interests aligned. The age of competition is over,
> the age of collaboration has begun."
> Dr. Bak Nguyen

So, can we come together with humility to rebuild with more flexibility and swiftness? Can we let go of our hypocrisy and our lies of perfection? For as long as we are still pretending to be perfect, we will turn a blinded eye to **humility, flexibility** and **adaptability**.

Collaboration does not mean to compromise but to build wiser and with better inclusion. Diversity was very trendy until COVID-19. Well it is not a trend, but a strength to be incorporated; and I am not talking about gender nor skin color, I am talking about our leaders of the difference of points of view.

Together with our difference, together with our common goal and liability, together as one. This is how we will prevail. This is how we will all survive. This is how we will prosper, as one. This is **RELEVANCY**.

Dr. BAK NGUYEN

CHAPTER 9
"LOOKING AT THE PAST TO GLIMPSE THE FUTURE"
by Dr. PAUL DOMINIQUE

"I see bubbles everywhere", said Nobel Laureate and Yale Professor of Economics Robert Schiller on October 23rd, 2019 to a group of investors in Los Angeles, referring to potential risk in the stock, bond, and housing markets. Schiller is held in high regard in the financial world as he had famously predicted the 2000 stock market crash and the 2007 housing crash that lead to the 2008 global financial crisis.

In this chapter I will describe why COVID-19 was simply the pin, albeit a harsh one, that burst what was possibly the largest economic bubble of my lifetime, and the future implications, with an emphasis on dental practice and my vision for the future of the profession.

At the time of Schiller's speech in 2019 the US economy was in the midst of the longest expansion since WWII, 126 months, which came to a halt with the onset of the COVID-19 pandemic.

According to the popular narrative, the American economy was enjoying its finest moment in history; after all, unemployment was at a record 50-year low and the Dow Jones Stock Index would ultimately go above 29,000 points on February 12th, 2020. It was the longest bull market in US history, running since March 11th, 2009 through two administrations at the Executive Branch and three Chairpersons at the US Federal Reserve Bank.

Despite this record expansion and the unprecedented bull stock market run, fundamental flaws were evident in the fabric of the US economy. There was a vocal minority of notable economists and financial luminaries who were going against the grain and signaling that such an expansion was built on a house of cards and that the mother of all crashes was in the making.

I started paying attention to them in the fall of 2016. The consensus among them was that we were **doomed to make the same mistakes** and we had not learned the lessons from the last financial crisis. Legendary investor and hedge fund manager Jim Rogers's premise is simple: the ultimate cause of the 2008 crisis was "too much debt and since then the debt has skyrocketed across the world".

David Stockman, who served under Ronald Reagan as Director of the Office of Management and Budget, shares Rogers's sentiments. He postulates that the American financial system has morphed into a demented bubble-prone gambling stage that erodes capitalistic prosperity and rewards speculators with large windfall gains. He argues that contrary to conventional wisdom, COVID-19 was a white swan rather than a black swan event.

The idea that central bankers can print their way out of economic pain through the issuance of debt is what ultimately leads to boom bust economic cycles; the creation of bigger debt bubbles as the proverbial can is kicked down the road. There is an inherent flaw in the federal reserve banking system and the fact that the US dollar enjoys reserve status is being overexploited.

Through unconventional monetary policy known as quantitative easing and the associated lowering of interest rates, the procurement of substantial debt was encouraged at all levels in the aftermath of the 2008 financial meltdown.

This was particularly evident in the corporate sector, where debt is approaching $10 trillion at the time of writing. Policy makers support the issuance of this colossal debt as in theory it is to be used for capital investment, expansion, job creation, and R&D; all with the goal of increasing the GDP through economic output.

However, what we have observed over the last decade is that a significant amount of this debt was funneled into stock buybacks, which was exacerbated with the 2018 corporate tax cuts. In plain words, what we observed was not the creation of abundance nor value nor jobs, but the feeding of an illusion of growth, one through debt. And the ball is always passed further down the road.

In 2019 JP Morgan estimated that almost a trillion dollars went into stock repurchases. The goal of these repurchases in one's own stock is to increase their companies share price without the corresponding growth in economic output; this practice was a major factor in driving the tremendous bull market.

This siphoning of money explains why we have mainly subpar GDP growth in the years subsequent to the great recession despite, then, record levels of stimulus being pumped into the U.S. economy. It also partially explains why, despite record job creation in the last several years, we observed wage stagnation, jobs not offering benefits, the rise of gig-workers and income inequality. In essence, the Fed is both the firefighter and the arsonist

Stock repurchases also lead to the overvaluation of other asset classes outside of equities, such as real estate via what behavioral economists refer to as the wealth effect. Consumers, particularly those who have a 401k or other retirement vehicles, feel more financially secure as they see their investment portfolios increase in value.

They feel wealthier even though their income remains the same and have the confidence to take on debt. This cycle of debt spirals uncontrollably through the economy and, as suggested above, leads to debt bubbles and overinflated asset classes. When the bubble finally bursts many consumers find themselves overleveraged and underwater.

Cracks were already beginning to emerge in 2019, where the auto industry reported that approximately 7 million Americans were more than 90 days delinquent on their auto loans.

We also saw bond market yield inversion in March of 2019, where the yield on 10-year Treasury bonds dipped below the 3-month Treasury bonds. This is typically a reliable prognosticator of an impending recession. Currently consumer debt approaching a colosal 14 Trillion.

Nouriel Roubini, Professor of Economics at New York University's Stern School of Business, was also sounding alarm bells over the last few years regarding the intensity of corporate and consumer debt levels. Roubini, like Schiller, is also credited with predicting the 2008 financial crisis. He is known for his rather sober outlook and this time he is rather gloomy in his sentiment. He is forecasting a **"U"-shaped** recovery post COVID-19 and will not rule out the risk of an **"L" shaped** or greater depression.

Because of the aforementioned debt levels, both households and corporations will enter a cycle of significant deleveraging and saving (due to uncertainty) causing a global investment slump, which is a recipe for an anemic recovery. He also claims that monetary and fiscal stimulus will not help, but serve to exacerbate current debt imbalances as rising debt levels explode.

While the largest corporations, and possibly some small business owners, will ultimately be bailed out by yet inflating another debt bubble, it remains to be seen who will come to the rescue of the over-leveraged consumer. Our patients fall mainly within the latter group and this will have significant implications for the dental profession going forward.

So how are we moving forward in a world with fewer and fewer means and with households topping their credit margin? This is not a trend, but the unveil of long lasting flaws and abuses of our economical status quo.

As dentists, we do not have the power to address such issues. Or have we? I truly believe that the first step is still to understand the waters we are bathing in, not even swimming.

We are highly educated and can read the charts and compile the numbers, if only, we know where to find them. Well, here they are, and feel free to research and to shape our view vision, but see the trend, see the bigger picture, one that is much bigger than our operatories.

This is how we will all survive. This is how we will prosper, as one. This is **RELEVANCY**.

Dr. BAK NGUYEN

CHAPTER 10
"DO IT BECAUSE YOU CAN"
by Dr. BAK NGUYEN

Paul has 75. Although he calls me a brother from another mother, I have the age to be his son. I reality appreciate the genuine friendship and how open he is and gives. While I am in my prime to make my mark, he is at the reflection of his legacy… but with the same excitement and intensity to write History, once more. This is what's keeping his relevancy.

Having written many books on the matter of our purpose and quest of identity, I can tell you that the answer can only be found from within. In other words, before we can fix our profession, we each must recognize our personal **VOID** first. We do not need to fix that void to fix our profession, but we must at least admit its existence.

Paul and I both have the same **VOID**. Because we were well aware of what was missing, we keep pushing forward. Paul is 75 and amongst one of the most positive person, I had the privilege to work within. He is positive and relevant because he is still looking forward with curiosity and ready to learn and to reinvent himself.

Don't be mistaken, Paul is a dragon in both dentistry and finance, having built multi-million dollars enterprises, but that's behind him. To Paul, it is all about what's next! Even at 75, especially at 75!

> "Relevancy is ahead, never behind."
> Dr. Bak Nguyen

If you were looking for a short way out of this chapter, that's your conclusion, to keep looking ahead! Like Paul, your past is experience and greats stories, but just keep what can be useful tomorrow and embrace the new, the day, the future.

The first time that Paul called me his brother from another mother, he said that he will be learning so much from me... I was uneasy. I responded genuinely that it as me that will be learning from him. Then, we agreed that we will be learning from each other. Those were the words, but in fact, we both knew that we will have fun from our conversation because it was based on openness and respect.

No, we are not building from the difference, we are pretty much alike, Paul and I. What's different is our experience and journey leading to our encounter. I had the chance to learn from him and quickly felt what he feels; as he is having a new thrill living his forties while keeping all of his wisdom and knowledge. That's how we both fill our **VOID**, finding a THOUGHT PARTNER to exchange and build with.

He is 75 and is very worried about the danger of the aerosol and the risk of contagion. I am too, but I am more concerned than afraid. That was truly the only reminder of our age difference. The relevancy of our friendship and partnership is based on our common interest to fill the **VOID** of our profession, looking ahead, with different toolset and skills.

He will tell you himself, as we are looking for ways to resume our profession, but better and with the least burden possible, not surrendering to fear and panic, we are finding our purpose looking for answers for our profession.

> "Give, gratitude and grow."
> Dr. Anil Gupta

Just like Dr. Anil Gupta prescribed with his **3G formula of immediate happiness**, GIVE - GRATITUDE - GROW, that's what we were doing, but without a formula. We gave what we had, embracing the day and ready to help, saying **YES**. That's how we opened up.

Then, we gave, not because we cared, because we could. That's your first trap, don't give because you care, that might take too much time to care. We gave immediately because we could, that's how we grew faster. In a nutshell, that's a great image to understand what relevancy is and how to rebuild our profession.

> "Give because you can, not because you care."
> Dr. Bak Nguyen

If you follow the same line of thoughts, the more you'll give, the more you'll grow. And trust me, you will feel that growth very quickly. What do you think that people like Paul and I are doing? We go out and test drive that new growth right away!

How do you test a newfound power? On the first available problem. Since our own problems are always harder to solve, we will apply it as someone is looking at us for help. And we will give again; give to grow once more. That's why we are always looking to the future because behind, there is nothing more we can do.

Now add to that the 3rd G: Gratitude. Trust me, that feeling is even better than the satisfaction to score! Why? Because no matter the result, we are sure of that great feeling from gratitude, the gratitude to have found our new power. Yup, even if we failed at the task, it was our first ride, the good feeling still stand. And by tomorrow, we will be better at it!

Hey, they were no expectation, since we didn't spend too much time thinking if we cared or not!

And with the power of Gratitude, we are once more empowered to give again. To give it a second chance, to give it one more try, to give it another day. By the second time, we are not expecting anything, we are simply re-aiming, having learned from the mistake me made yesterday. And, once again, because we acted swiftly, everything is still clear in our mind, easing the re-adjusting without the involvement of too much emotions.

Usually, by the second or the third time, we get it right. Because we acted and reacted so quickly, it also means that people didn't even see our mistake. As they were looking for the first steps, we were already at the final and had a victory to present. Once more, more gratitude and more growth, ready to give again!

If you wanted my power of momentum, my speed, Paul's optimism and ageless energy combined with the wisdom and resilience of Anil, we just gave you the formula and how to apply it. Say **YES**. Do it because you can, not because you care. Feel the difference inside and keep pushing! It can be as simple as that.

And what about that **VOID**? Well, that **VOID** was a lack of vision and leadership. One can stand for eternity scratching his head for answers he does not know, or he can be running looking for what he does not know. The only way to know is to try. And the easiest way to try is to do, right away! So do to feel, do because you can, do while you still can. The longer you wait, the harder it will be!

Oh, and what about solving other's people problem before solving our own? Is that ethical? As a medical and dental doctor, we should know better! No one can operate on him/herself. It is even forbidden to operate on our relatives and people we care for emotionally. It might affect our judgement. Well, that we got right! Apply the same principle to the rest of life.

> "The skills are within, the subject is ahead, in front of you."
> **Dr. Bak Nguyen**

Don't try to operate on our problems, you are the last person qualified to do so. Help others to solve their problems. Even if they don't help you in return, you will have learned and grown enough to overcome your own. That's how Paul and I grew stronger and wiser, ahead of the curve. We grew because we could. Then, we cared.

I am not playing with the words here. If anything, I look back telling you how to order the steps in an efficient way. When you think of it, nothing is really new here, and yet, so many are failing, so many intelligent and smart people. That's because the narrative was beautiful, but never, they got the order in which to apply the formula.

I was doing it without being aware. It is only after talking with Anil more than once that I understood where I stood in his system. This is my twist, looking at Paul and at myself. I could keep going on and on about the quest of identity, but time isn't on our side. I will refer you to my previous books on the matter.

> "Do it because you can, not because you care."
> Dr. Bak Nguyen

Try it today. Only once you have recognized your imperfection and **VOID**, will you act. Do not operate on your own problems, but be kind enough to help someone else. The kindness was to yourself!

Then act and react fast, since there were no expectations and you weren't emotionally invested, you can feel the gratitude of a new power emerging. Let that feeling empower you and come back at the problem the next day. Soon enough, you will have grown much, no matter your age.

The vision was to help the other. The leadership was to do it right away and with it, the **power of GRATITUDE** will empower your growth to soon overcome your own **VOID**.

Put that back into context with what my friend and mentor Christian Trudeau was saying: stay humble, check; be flexible, check; be swift, check! Now, you are ready to rebuild our profession, now you are relevant.

This is how we will prevail. This is how we will all survive. This is how we will prosper, as one. This is **RELEVANCY**.

Dr. BAK NGUYEN

CHAPTER 11
"THE OUELLETTE LEGACY"
by Dr. PAUL OUELLETTE

I am soon to be 76-years YOUNG in July of this year. Am I ready to slow down and smell the roses? Maybe. I have a 5-year plan. The problem I have with retirement is that I am addicted to learning and sharing.

My retirement dream would be to travel the world lecturing about Orthodontics and Implant Dentistry. My wife and her sister Jeanette, also love to travel. Their favorite means of traveling was to see the world on a cruise ship. The Pandemic has sadly changed this for all seniors.

At our ages, it may now be too risky to place ourselves in confined spaces for long periods of time. Social distancing and travel by car are now recommended for seniors. However, I do not consider myself a Senior!

The Ouellette Family's Legacy started with my mother Lanette Ouellette. She is currently 96 years old. In today's marketing-driven society you could say she invented **THE OUELLETTE BRAND** What is the Ouellette brand? Our family has ingrained in their DNA the following personality traits.

A GENE FOR GIVING

It is better to be a giver than a taker! Giving back to the community is the foundation of the family brand. This includes giving back to our profession. Mentoring and teaching young people is part of it too. Growing up we watched Mama Lanette volunteer for many causes. No matter how small or insignificant the cause, she was an organizer and caregiver to those in need. She always said **YES**!

A GENE FOR KINDNESS

Kindness comes easy to the Ouellette family. We have the reputation of always being friendly, generous and considerate of other people. Sometimes this quality might be deemed naïve or weak. This is definitely not the case!

Often it takes courage and strength to remember to be kind and to understand all people. You may encounter people that are negative and very rude. Just smile and LISTEN to what they're saying. You may not agree, but you have not made an enemy.

It may take a while for a new patient or acquaintance to warm up to you. Earn their trust and you may be surprised to make a new friend that at first, was cautious and reserved.

"Win your friends with kindness."
Dr. Paul Ouellette

THE COMPASSION GENE

If one is compassionate, he/she has an innate willingness to help others. This is a word for a very positive emotion that makes you thoughtful and decent. You put yourself into their shoes and try to feel their pain or concerns.

> "Compassion is the true love of doing something for others."
> **Dr. Paul Ouellette**

Empathy can be compared to compassion. Empathy is the ability to actually be in the shoes of the other person. It is as if you feel their pain as well. A biblical quote defines it:

> "Speak up for those who cannot speak for themselves, for the rights of all who are destitute. Speak up and judge fairly; defend the rights of the poor and needy." – Proverbs 31:8-9, NIV

It's helpful to have this mindset when consulting with new patients and making new acquaintances.

THE BEING FOCUSED GENE

Being focused means that you have your eye on the ball! You are laser-focused on your goals and objectives. You completely commit to achieving those goals and objectives no matter what.

I learned how to focus and concentrate as one of my first goals, back when I was a teenager. I wanted to pursue a career in dentistry. My journey to becoming an orthodontist started at age 14. I had the opportunity to be treated by one of the most famous orthodontists in the world, Dr. Joseph Jarabak.

Our family could not afford braces at the time. My mother took me to Loyola School of Dentistry in downtown Chicago. I was accepted into their clinic and the resident that manage my case was Dr.Don Hilgers. He was one of my first role models. Drs. Hilgers and Jarabak encouraged and motivated me to stay focused. Ten years later, I graduated from Loyola as an orthodontist.

Dr Jarabak retired and Dr. Hilgers became the Chairman of the Orthodontic Department. My dreams as a teenage became reality as I was **LASER-FOCUSED**.

THE ETHICAL GENE

My mother has always **walked the walk**, showing us by example, the benefits of following good moral standards, always being truthful, fair to all and honest. The dental school I attended in Chicago taught us the same values as Mama Lanette. We use our inherited trait every day when we meet new patients and work with our team members.

THE TRUTH GENE

Truth matters! First, be truthful to yourself. Be truthful to your family, colleagues and patients. You **can't go wrong always trying to do the right thing** for everyone.

And if you do that, you'll be doing the right thing for yourself. We do not focus solely on money and profit when we consult and treat our patients. If we do a good job success and financial rewards naturally come, both to us as individuals and to society as a whole.

As individuals, being truthful means that we can mature always learning from our mistakes. Our Western society places a high value on truth in advertising and performing our jobs ethically. Surround yourself with like-minded team members. Your patients, friends and family will see you succeed beyond your expectations. That is the **TRUTH gene**!

THE STRATEGIC LENIENCY GENE

One of the things I learned when developing more than 35 dental practices over a 49 years career was how to **lead by example**. I did not always make the right choices and sometimes hired a team member that did not initially live up to our organization's minimal standards.

As a rule, I do not immediately fire the person. That may have been the best and most prudent decision. Perhaps my training team and I failed the new employee. I believe everyone deserves a 2nd chance and sometimes we need to work harder to bring that person around. The **Compassion Gene** in our DNA also helped.

We are all human and not always perfect, especially me. I would put myself in his or her shoes. I would ask myself did the employee intentionally not follow our protocols, make frequent excuses or worse, not be truthful?

I learned from an Oral Surgeon, Dr. Louis Belinfante to always use "Strategic Leniency" first! Following his advice, The Dental Specialists Central Florida aka TDS, created the finely tuned TDS Dream Team.

THE OUELLETTE LEGACY

Observe other people's feelings.
Put yourself in their shoes.
Unconditional respect for family,
Friends and others should always be in mind.
Excitement and passion for life, ALWAYS.
Love God.

Live your life to the fullest!
Energy is always positive.
Avoid negative thoughts.
Trust in God.

Treat friends, family and others
As you would want to be treated.
Responsible carefully planned decisions
Ethical behavior make great leaders.
Share these traits with everyone
In your sphere of influence.

We are the **OUELLETTE FAMILY** of dentists and this is our **LEGACY BLUEPRINT.**

This is how we will all survive. This is how we will prosper, as one. This is **RELEVANCY**.

Dr. BAK NGUYEN

CHAPTER 12

"THE TIME FOR HALF MEASURES IS OVER"
by Dr. BAK NGUYEN

The **GREAT DENTAL DEPRESSION**. That's not me talking, it is Paul. I am pretty good with words, but I have to admit how on point and accurate Paul is with the **GREAT DENTAL DEPRESSION**.

We both saw it coming since the beginning o the confinement, the **GREAT PAUSE**. Well, we know that our economy and the world economy is under pressure and there will be side effects. The virus will have its casualties, and the collaterals will not rank in the million but hundreds of billion.

Most economists and experts are predicting the extinction of maybe 50% of the small businesses and a difficult 2020 and 2021. Well, that is an understatement for our industry, the dental industry. In the USA, the big dental corporations with their huge overheads are already showing signs of weakness.

In Canada and France, where the boutique clinics are dominant, most of these small businesses are on the shoulder of individuals that may or may not survive this crisis. The **GREAT PAUSE** was only the beginning, the worse is what will be following.

We are still in the midst of the **GREAT PAUSE** at the time of this writing. What is coming next is too obvious to ignore. From both sides of the ocean, French, Americans, Peruvians and Canadians all agreed on the difficult times ahead.

One because of our poor relevancy leading to a weak voice in society. Two, because under the new reign of **FEAR**, clinical protocols will be tighten and more costly then never before... and we were already too expensive as a profession before COVID-19!

Three, with patients losing their jobs and the insecurity ahead, who will be running back at the dentist for a cleaning or for braces? It is likely that many of the dental clinics might go under... unless we stand together, unless we redefine our place and relevancy before the end of the **GREAT PAUSE**.

How many times were we given the chance to prepare for what is coming? How many times, we had so much time to understand. Sure, the first two weeks were unreal and denials, but now, it is time to face the music and to look up, not down on our bellybutton.

To an unprecedented crisis, forget the half measures. Even this morning, I woke up reading articles and press reports on the national debt ratio and the deficit ahead. Those who think that we can be conservative and reasonable, they are in for a wild, very wild ride.

Just like in the aftermath of the the second great war, everything will have to be redefined, everything has changed forever. For the better or for worse, it is still for us to decide, now that we are still living the **GREAT PAUSE**.

As a society, debt was already a commodity, now, it will be your salvation for the foreseeable future. If you can borrow, do it before it is gone. Borrow and restructure. And what about reimbursing? Well, for as long as you still can reimburse, that will means that you got to the other side.

Just like Paul went from under and emerged victorious from the 2008 recession, if you act swiftly, you will make it out alive, different and, hopefully, even wiser and stronger. But that was just the first patch, the quick fix.

How about our relevancy? Is 3% acceptable to you? Is being put on the sideline and blindly obeying the directives of the central power acceptable to any of you? We can do better, we have to do better. Legacy, relevancy, we need to redefine our role and place in the new society.

What would that be? I won't overstep my place to impose my views. This is a dialogue that we all must engage in, as soon as possible. But how that will take place, that I can tell you.

> "The time for half measures is over."
> Dr. Bak Nguyen

This crisis will have cost so much that after the death count, it will be the reign of **FEAR**. History has taught us more than once the usual casualties: **FREEDOM** and **INDIVIDUAL RIGHTS**. In the name of public protection, of public health, what will be imposed next? What restriction will not be lifted?

What usually follows **FEAR** are intolerance and paranoia… until greed and hunger for power take over. Can we do better? Can we stop History from repeating itself? Before you tell me how alarmist and farfetched this is, consider the fact that no one could have ever predicted that all of the world will be standing still, all at once.

Now, even fever are comprehending the long term consequences of the virus and of our reaction… these record deficits are nearly the tip of the iceberg. It will get worse, much worse before it will get better.

This is barely within 2 months of the war… and no one knows when the siege will end. Because yes, worse than a war, this is a siege, where the only win is to lose big or to lose it all. There won't be any **spoil of war** here!

And yes, we will survive and prevail. Many, not all of us, but we will make it. But to what end? And to what destination? Those are my question to you, doctors.

> "COVID-19 also killed complacency, moderation and conservatism. Now it is about overachieving and dialogue."
> Dr. Bak Nguyen

In my previous chapters, I revealed ways to make it through the glass ceiling, to the other side, borrowing from Paul's past. Now, on the other side, to be part of the new world order, we will need to redefine our relevancy very, very quickly.

To that end, I brought in **THE ALPHAS**, those forward thinkers and overachievers who win and score because of who they are and what they are made of.

I am hosting the **OVERACHIEVERS** summit at the **INTERNATIONAL DENTAL SUMMIT**. Not to brag our past and achievements. I am applauding those peers coming out to share their mindset and secrets to move forward, together.

> "The age of competition is over,
> the age of collaboration is now, or no one
> will be left to hear any other title."
> Dr. Bak Nguyen

These overachievers are not given the floor because they overachieved, but because they are overachieving and will continue to do so. Just like any distribution curve, those are the ones ahead.

But are we all, at some point, in the top tier of the distribution curve? Haven't we leverage ourselves up from our competing spirit? Natural and academic selection brought us together. It is time to leverage that!

It is with that idea that I brought the **OVERACHIEVERS** summit, a first of its kind and a beacon that I hope will attract the interest of the other **ALPHAS** out there. And the public?

As doctors, we are all **ALPHAS**, some are just more verbal than others. But from our training and the **VOID**, the lack of vision and leadership, we leverage those skills to differentiate amongst us while we should have connected and built from its synergy.

Well, it is now or never. The time for half measures is over. It is do or die… or survive to endure. If we do not have a voice within the next few months, we will have to obey and to endure. We are expected to obey!

Well, I will obey, but first, I will put the table for dialogues and leverage the intelligence of our profession, the elite character of its selection and leverage upon the given time of the **GREAT PAUSE**. For as long as I lead **THE ALPHAS**, I will not tell any of you what to do but will encourage each of you to join the dialogue.

All I can do is to inspire and to empower, it will be up to you to decide. To all the **ALPHAS** out there looking to join the conversation and the initiative, here is my promise to all and each one of you: I do not care if we agree or not. I do not even care if we stand on opposite views.

What I will defend and empower is a logic and a line of thoughts that can be followed and debated. For as long as you believe in your values and ideas, and can clearly express them for a better collective future, you will have the floor.

The **OVERACHIEVERS** are opening the march looking to share and to inspire. But alone, and few, our voice and influence will be absorbed and assimilated by bigger organizations. If there is a time to keep our best within our ranks, it is now, as we are setting the tables for real dialogues, driven by change, not titles and labels.

Left, right, capitalist, socialist, an **ALPHA** is an **ALPHA**. With the chance of dialogue and a system of co-presidency, both liable for the actions of the other, we can emerge victorious of this siege. We can have our voice, the **spoils of war** will be coming from all the waste resources within our systems, those we spend fighting amongst ourselves.

We can and we will build from the difference! Not with opposition, not with resistance, but with synergy and creativity, with tolerance and collaboration.

"It is time to move DIVERSITY from trend to value. And once again, I am not talking about gender, race or age."
Dr. Bak Nguyen

Where to go, we will figure it out together, if you join the dialogue. How to go, is ahead and with full strength. This is not the excitement or the opportunity of a revolution, this is not a smooth evolution, this is the world post-COVID-19.

Will we have our voice and place within the new world? It is up to our **RELEVANCY**. This is not about power or influence, but about being active or passively obey and endure. It is time to rebuild, will you lend a hand?

This is how we will prevail. This is how we will all survive. This is how we will prosper, as one. This is **RELEVANCY**.

Dr. BAK NGUYEN

CHAPTER 13
"THE DOMINIQUE INITIATIVE"
by Dr. PAUL DOMINIQUE

The COVID-19 crisis is taking the global financial system into uncharted waters once more, and with it our patients. The pandemic also raises possible infection control issues within our profession.

Will patients feel safe visiting the dentist? Will they have the means to do so? The answer to the latter question is purely dependent on the state of the economy, and recent historical industry-specific data may not offer promising news.

Just like in other industries, most U.S. based dentists experienced a downturn during the last recession. However, data from the American Dental Association's (ADA) chief economist, Marco Vujicic, demonstrates the decline actually started in 2003, but the overall trend was masked significantly by variation in age and income level of patients.

While there was a steady increase in the utilization among children, there was a pronounced drop in the utilization among non-elderly adults, with the exception of the wealthiest income group. This contraction among adults was noted to date back to 1997.

According to the Health Policy Institute (HPI) of the ADA, in 2015 only 36% of U.S. adults (19-64yrs) visited a dentist in the preceding 12 months. For seniors it was 43.7% and for children (under 19yrs), 48.5%. Bottom line, **less than half** of the U.S. population visit a dentist on an annual basis. The cost of care is often cited as to why utilization is so sub-optimal.

In 2016, an HPI study reported that dentistry has the highest level of cost barriers compared to other health care services, such as prescription drugs, medical care, eyeglasses, and mental health services. This has some significant repercussions for morbidity issues in our profession and HPI data is startling.

> On average, every 15 seconds someone visits a hospital emergency department for dental issues.

In 2017 there were 2.1 million emergency room visits for dental conditions and, outside of normal business hours, 70% of all emergency department visits were related to dental problems. The total cost of these visits was **2.7 billion** in 2017.

This is a shocking revelation: U.S. hospitals are billing more for dental health conditions than the largest DSO on the planet. How many hospitals employ dentists or even have dental handpieces and other dental related equipment?

Despite serving less than half of the U.S. population, as dentists, we enjoy some of highest remuneration nationally. However, according to data from the ADA, there has been a slide in inflation adjusted net income for general dentists that, just like adult utilization, preceded the great recession of 2008.

Dental care utilization patterns in America are clearly changing, they are changing in very different ways for children and for adults and the effects are being seen in the net income reported by generalists.

The dichotomy we are observing is coincident with the fact that more and more children are being insured through state sponsored insurance plans while adult dental benefits are eroding. In 2018, just over a third of general dentists reported an increase in patient volume compared to the previous year.

Looking into the future, it is not difficult to foresee that this decline for adults will continue. We are at a critical moment in our profession, given the profound economic challenges on the horizon and that this is coincident with eroding adult dental benefits.

This is a defining moment for dentistry and according to Marko Vujicic et al. now is not the **time for complacency** as we run the risk of "ceding control of our profession to others." To a certain extent one can make the case that we are already experiencing this within the clear aligner segment of the orthodontic market.

Prior to COVID-19, the U.S. economy was decoupling from China. The pandemic will expedite this process and will result in significant supply chain disruptions. This will deliberately drive innovation in order to offset the higher salaries of U.S. workers, and we have seen examples of this in the past where there was a significant wage gap between two sovereign economies.

In modern terms, we can expect an acceleration of automation, digitization and robotization in many of the affected industries and this will have a spillover effect into healthcare, including dentistry, similar to what we are seeing with 3D printing and orthodontics.

The initiative I would like to drive, going forward out of this pandemic is the digitization of oral hard and soft tissue structures that we treat. In other words, I would like to see a profession-driven revolution in teledentistry.

Through the use of high-resolution intraoral cameras, digital radiography, digital infrared trans-illumination (CariVu) and 3D intraoral scanning, we can complete a very accurate dental exam on a patient from anywhere in the world.

Currently researchers at the University of San Diego are developing a probing free method to measure periodontal pocket depths. The system involves the patient rinsing with a squid ink solution that is taken up into the gingival sulcus via capillary action. The squid ink has light-absorbing nanoparticles that can ultimately be detected, thus allowing pocket depth to be measured comfortably and with no ambivalence.

My vision is the creation of dental imaging centers where the above technologies are available to the public and these facilities are staffed by technical operators such as dental assistants. These centers would be best located in areas of high foot traffic for convenience, such as pharmacies, university health centers, large corporate centers, etc. and they can potentially be pop-up. Such innovation would allow dentists and hygienists to virtually gather the data they need for accurate diagnosis at substantial savings to the patient.

A significant part of my initiative is reform in dental hygiene. The current one-size-fits-all approach to hygiene is fundamentally flawed. The merging of teledentistry with hygiene services makes tremendous sense, as it allows for continuous caries risk assessment leading to individualized prophylactic recall visits.

The etiology of dental caries is the demineralization of tooth structure from the metabolic activity of plaque bacteria. Through the use of simple disclosing solution and accurate high definition intraoral photography, dentists and hygienists can frequently monitor and update a patient's caries risk, thus customizing their recall frequency rather than using the standard twice a year approach.

This novel preventative-based approach will reduce the need for restorative care and will make the existing model obsolete over time due to less morbidity and patient savings. We will have the capability to raise a generation of subscribers who can be caries free through frequent tele-examination combined with individualized professional biofilm management.

Tyto Care (tytocare.com) is an Israeli company that also operates in the U.S. It allows patients to perform professionally guided medical exams from the comfort of their home. They sell FDA approved user-friendly diagnostic medical devices to consumers, such as otoscopes, thermometers, stethoscope adaptors, etc.

Parents who have acquired these devices have reported a dramatic reduction in ER visits for their children. Therefore, it's not too far-fetched to imagine that the devices I mentioned above, from the imaging centers, will one day be available in the homes of consumers.

I realize that the last couple of paragraphs are probably anxiety provoking to most dentists reading this. For those who feel this way, I would like to stress that this is a process that will take time to execute and refine in order to attain the desired preventative approach to the masses.

In the interim, the dental imaging centers will be proven to be an invaluable asset to most practices as it will expose significant existing disease. Imagine the power of being able to have an online database of potential patients, treatment plan remotely and discuss professional fees all before the patient presents to the office.

The ramifications are enormous: dentists can search for conditions they prefer to treat, collaborate with colleagues online for complex multidisciplinary cases, present treatment plan options that suit the patient's budget and so on. The efficiencies created through this approach will result in more **productive chair time**, which translates into savings and increased profits.

Furthermore, dentists who are able to recruit and treatment plan virtually may no longer need to own a brick and mortar facility, as they may be able to rent chair time as per demand, leading to a different business model.

The world is changing, and the aftermath of COVID-19 will be an impetus to accelerate the pace of change. Those of us who are prepared to embrace the coming technological shifts and facilitate them will not only thrive but will handsomely profit, ethically, in the post pandemic era.

> "See the past, embrace the shift
> and you won't be left behind."
> **Dr. Paul Dominique**

It is still a choice we all must make. This is how we will prevail. This is how we will all survive. This is how we will prosper, as one. This is **RELEVANCY**.

Dr. BAK NGUYEN

CHAPTER 14
"3% RELEVANCY"
by Dr. BAK NGUYEN

Yesterday I hosted the **OVERACHIEVERS'** summit. It was simply eye-opening. Eye-opening because we could have done this ages ago, but we were all too busy proving that we were better than those standing beside us.

Sure, the need for differentiation rid us hard and pushed us to surpass ourselves within the tracks of our vision, leaving behind the essence of being a doctor in medical science: warmth and humanity.

Don't get me wrong, I had much fun exchanging freely and openly with peers and thinkers willing to share their thoughts to advance the average, yes, not only for ourselves but to move the average up. The corruption of the elite is as such:

> "We spent our entire life trying to beat the average, now, in a leadership position, our role is to fight to raise the average."
> Dr. Bak Nguyen

Not all leaders are equal, not all leaders are good, despite their tongue. I started this book laughing with Paul, on the quote that a leader needs a big heart.

Then, Anil joined and showed us the map with his **3G (Give - Gratitude - Growth)**. Eric was moving heaven and earth to keep his philanthropic efforts alive and Paul explained his addiction.

Paul Dominique struggled to find the right wording to formulate his proposal to fight the injustice, using technology to prevent dental illness, but all along, he was right and was a much needed forward thinker.

Joining in were two new Alphas, Eric Pulver and Nach Daniel, two oral surgeons heavily invested in artificial intelligence to the next age of relevancy of dentistry. We all came together and shared our vision for the future, our hope for relevancy. Our engagement to break the glass ceiling, enough to let you through, all of you. And then, to rebuild on the other side.

In the past, a talk like this would only happen behind close doors and amongst highly referred individuals. There will be talks and debates, and one of the smartest mind in the room will find a flaw throwing everything back to the floor. This is why, most Alphas worked quietly in their corner of the world, gathering their own team and leading their own charge.

Even if each of the Alphas has enough strength and conviction to make it through the glass ceiling, on the other side, they will be irrelevant, standing alone, naked.

"The Virus showed us who vulnerable we really are, with 3% relevancy or less!"
Dr. Bak Nguyen

Most of the conversation went around technology and how to apply it. In the past, our profession (average) was protected with a **legal monopoly**. Well, the advancement of technology and the democratization of our society showed us how that is a relic of the past that can no longer serve as a shield.

Then, the virus came, showing our vulnerability, even to socialist states where the are no competition amongst peer-dentist, France. That's a country where dentists are so loved that they are elected as mayors! We don't see that on this side of the ocean. Nonetheless, their relevancy went down to **3%** or less, being set aside as soon as the war was declared.

Dr. Dominique's proposal to target the illness at its source, using teledentistry and lowering the cost of care made much, much sense. But even if we debated this privately before, we were both very concerned about how the message will be received by a crowd of dentists!

Well, the Alphas embraced the idea, saying that this is the future, once we will be building from the glass ceiling and up.

How? It was still for all of us to figure out, but you can't oppose technology and progress. That we saw, that we learned.

As Dr. Pulver and Dr. Daniel were looking at means to implement the technological component to it, Dr. Lacoste was addressing the logic of accessible and affordable cares, but with the fear that our profession will not be moving in that direction, at least from our lifetime.

That's where I brought my expertise to the mix. If we are vouching to fight to lower the cost of our profession, I could make it work! Finally, something I could rally the people around! And then, to convince the rest of the dental profession to join will not be that difficult.

If anything, **COVID-19** caught all of the dental clinics, big and small, exposed and unprepared. Many of these clinics are under immense financial pressure and might go under, that we all know.

Well, add to that the scarcity of the patients at the return (3% relevancy will grow, but hardly back to 100% within the following months). Combined this and the new norms and safety regulation for sterilization (evaluated at approximatively 20-25% of the actual infrastructures) and you understand the extinction-level pressure that we are facing.

So, even if we brought back our relevancy thanks to the **OUELLETTE INITIATIVE**, that will only be the bridge to the other side. That's the **quick fix**. Then, we still have to heavily invest to be **COVID** safe, being already handicapped by the financial consequences of the **GREAT PAUSE**.

Do you see the problem? First of all, we have too many infrastructures on the ground. Because of the abundance of infrastructures, we will have to invest ridiculous amounts of money, and to what end? To keep competing one against the other. In the past, at least, we were helping the economy with our expenses; nowadays, we might kill it.

How do you expect the world's production to build as many specific equipment to meet the dental global demand? We are creating an artificial shortage, just like with the shortage of respirators, masks and medical wears within the war.

Eventually, this might serve a new emerging industry, but have we forgot something, someone? What about the general public? Who will be paying for that extra investment? The dentists will be the first to pay, then, if they are not going under, will transfer the bill to their patients; and our cares will be even less accessible! If you've followed the thought process of our relevancy, that how we came to **3%**!

Dr. Lacoste even outlined the phenomena, with the advent of so many new technologies in the dental field, the fees were not coming down, there were rising instead! Why? Because of the waste and abundance in infrastructures deployed on the field. What dental clinics run 24/7? And yet, the equipment is there, dormant and piling up the compound interests. And then, it will need to be upgraded!

If we keep following that path, our profession might not see another decade before the people will find a way to replace most of us, not because we did a poor job, but because they couldn't get to us!

I told you how we got stuck at the **glass ceiling** because we were too busy fighting amongst ourselves. Well, here's a clarification: we were too busy focusing on production to pay the compounded interest and the waste of our **VOID**. This has to change, right now.

We must learn to share and to listen more. This is only to help the average of our ranks to update their mindset to get through the glass ceiling. And then, how about Dr. Dominique's proposal?

Well, if you've done the math as many time as I have, you will understand how cheaper it will be for any of you to service in your operatories, only those with real surgical needs, not preventions nor minor cares. The cost/revenue ratio simply does not add up!

I proposed, a few years ago, to get out of the operatory as many treatments as possible, with my **Mdex**'s offers. Now, the virus is pushing the philosophy for me. But that will simply be the first ground.

What Dr. Dominique is proposing is to use teledentistry and distance monitoring to serve prevention. This isn't a threat to our profession! If anything, it is a blessing! Will you keep seeing a patient for 30 minutes for prevention while that may have costed you $300-$400/hour in production and cost? Could you charge that child $200? Of course not!

This is still the genesis of the dialogue, but one mandatory if we want to keep and raise our relevancy: to lower the fees, to increase accessibility and to cut the waste in infrastructures.

I wasn't smart enough to think of that solution. Paul Dominique was. But with my logic and eloquence, we put a summit together and got other great minds to contribute. The **ALPHAS** showed up.

I wasn't smart nor experienced enough to find a bridge through the glass ceiling. Paul Ouellette was. His past is our immediate salvation. And yet, only as we came together as **ALPHAS**, we had a chance to bring the initiative to your awareness, to the next level.

I wasn't kind enough to find a way to leverage our society through this crisis. Eric Lacoste challenged me and together, we wrote a *manifesto*, **AFTERMATH**, showing all corporations and big organization a way to leverage their way out of this mess, one that will be sustainable and profitable, not leaving anyone behind.

And then, Anil Gupta simplified the equation for us, with **3G, Give, Gratitude, Grow**. Does this make more sense now?

> "As a cosmetic dentist, I learned to listen to my patients and stopped locking down on them, telling them what they need."
> Dr. Bak Nguyen

Well, the spirit of the **OVERACHIEVERS Summit** was to break the ice of the **new age of collaboration** in the dental field. We were all prepared to be squeezed out of our secrets and leverages to help the profession, the average. This was in good sport.

Well, Dr. Lacoste threw me under the bus, even with a friendly tone, asking me how could I find relevancy between caring for dental health and cosmetic treatments. That took me by surprise and completely off guard! I was already sharing my numbers and company's leverage, but I wasn't expecting that curved ball.

Well, I answered without thinking much: since the day I became a cosmetic surgeon, I became loved and respected by my patients. I did so because I learned to listen to their desires and delivered on them with my skills and confidence.

My **relevancy** was found from my **humility** to stop looking down on my patients to tell them what they need but to listen instead. That's what I meant saying:

> "I treat people, not teeth."
> Dr. Bak Nguyen

What started as a curved ball, became a home run. Even if I wrote that times and times again in my books and even on my operatory, (yes, there are quotes of mine all throughout my clinics, written over glass walls) I never had the chance to articulate it on a table of peers, of **ALPHAS**.

Just like I promised you, I would not be lecturing you on what to do. I will only share with you what I did, how and why. Well, I did ask Eric to fill in the host role and to squeeze me out of my secrets. I did not expect that one, but it came out stronger and better than I would have ever imagined. Earlier, Christian Trudeau, my mentor, told us to be humble and flexible.

Well, to stop looking down on our patients is the first lesson of **humility**. Just that should raise our relevancy by a few points. Then, by being open to come and help, even if we aren't convinced, but simply because we can, that's **flexibility**. That's what happened on the Summit on Dr. Dominique's initiative: to lower the cost of dental care!

The third advice from M. Trudeau was to **adapt swiftly**. Well, that one, we will have to work all together as one to figure it out! But if I've learned one thing from the journey of the **ALPHAS**, is that perfection is only a lie, it is a perversion. Think of it for a second, what is perfection? Is it science, craft, skills?

> "Since it is not true, perfection is pure pride!"
> Dr. Bak Nguyen

That's what kept us for humility, from flexibility, from adaptability… until our relevancy dropped to **3%**! In a way, **THE VIRUS** might have saved our profession, if we awake now.

> "The Alphas aren't just overachievers, they are here because they are overachieving and will keep doing so."
> Dr. Bak Nguyen

And who will be leading the charge? You! As the **ALPHAS** were nothing but the first who stood up, others will have to join and to push further, bolder with an event bigger hearts and even broader minds.

The **glass ceiling** has broken and the hole is huge. Take our hands and cross the bridge of the **OUELLETTE INITIATIVE** to safer grounds. Join in the **Mdex & Co** and the **LACOSTE INITIATIVE** to keep your overhead and production cost down. Then, come and share the dialogue of the **DOMINIQUE INITIATIVE** to lower the cost of dental care.

What am I? What are we? We are the **INITIATIVES**. I am, you are, we are **ALPHAS**. This is how we will prevail. This is how we will all survive. This is how we will prosper, as one. This is **RELEVANCY**.

Dr. BAK NGUYEN

CHAPTER 15
"THE LACOSTE INITIATIVE"
by Dr. ERIC LACOSTE

It is generally accepted that **Relevancy** is the state of being closely connected to the matter at hand. I always wanted to be relevant to a point where it became an important driving force inside almost an obsession. I want to leave no doubt about the relevancy of my actions, my mission as a father, coach, role model, community leader and businessman.

I believe that when the end of one's journey comes, he or she will be remembered for everything that defines his or her accomplishments more than by the final number on their bank statement. Exceptional individuals are remembered by their relevancy with their family, their friends, their communities and the world.

Relevancy, is a state of being that requires authenticity as it allows to be seen without pretense, without phoniness, completely genuine. It requires mastery of an art or a level of competence, skills and execution that not only constantly defy the status quo but also push the accepted boundaries. Finally, it requires being humble, empathic and open as such values pave the way to your essential bond with others.

For the most part of the past two decades, I have been pursuing my quest to achieve relevancy. While learning from my failures and fueling off my wins, I continuously moved toward this somewhat elusive wondering what its true essence really was.

November 27th 2019, I received the Homage award from the Board of Dentists of Quebec, becoming the youngest ever to receive such peer's recognition. A little before, in 2018, I received The Telus social implication award as well as my second Dunamis award given by the Laval chamber of commerce. By measurable metrics, I was well on my way to completing this quest of relevancy or was I?

March 15th 2020 came the **GREAT PAUSE**, day 1. It is the day I learned that my clinic would be shut down. It is also the day where most of my means to be involved in my community took a great hit. Soon after, I would come to realize that it is also the day that would mark the beginning of redefining the meaning of relevancy. In the coming days, all would be redefined.

Strangely, I did not really feel anxious, or worried. I stayed calm and planned to make the most of the **time off**. It was a unique opportunity to reconnect with the essential, my three boys who I draw a lot of my inspiration from: Olivier, Matis and Nathan. It was also a great opportunity to optimize my workout regimen as well as my eating habits.

At 47 years old, I decided I would work out with the goal to meet the Navy SEAL PST Standards and so I did. The first few days of the great pause allowed me to relax my mind, to reflect and also to heal some of the wear and tear caused by our crazy schedules. I also took the time to reconnect with family and friends.

Without any success, I repeatedly offered my services to join the effort in the fight against the coronavirus. As the situation evolved, I realized that it was too early to draw an effective business strategy for the comeback. Then a question came to mind!

Did I simply want to come back or did I want to contribute to a movement of sustainable change, an opportunity to redefine society and maybe even the world as we know it?

> "A winner is a dreamer who never gives up."
> Nelson Mandela

I would never pretend that I have the answers on what it takes to change the world but making one change at a time with the hope of influencing others, maybe I could contribute. With this in mind, I started to reach out to whoever would be interested to exchange ideas not knowing where this would lead me.

MY PREMISE

I genuinely care for others, of my sons, my family, my staff, my patients and anyone who I can help in my community.

Whatever actions I was going to take would have to be in line with this premise.

Professionally, I strongly believed that nothing but verified information should be disseminated and I was not going to derive from this principle. Although my clinic was effectively closed going from 30+ patients a day to approximately 3 a month, I would still be loyal to my business model and beliefs. Years ago, I incorporated social corporate responsibility as a pillar of my operations and I would need to find a way to keep this alive.

> "True leaders make time to help others even when they are hurt themselves."
> Dr. Eric Lacoste

THE ALPHAS

Dr. Bak Nguyen reached out to me on LinkedIn. Eligibly, he asked me to share my views on the future of our industry. I accepted not suspecting that not only I would find a true friend but that we would quickly challenge each other to write a book about all of this in the matter of two weeks.

More importantly, the message would resonate, be relevant and in line the **United Nations Global Compact Initiative**. The records will show that it is exactly what happened! Three weeks later **AFTERMATH, Business after the Great Pause** was printed and for sale on Amazon.

Better yet, what started as a crazy idea would also serve a critical purpose to me: all the proceeds, his and mine, would go to support my mission of helping the underprivileged children of Laval, my community. Suddenly things were aligning.

Working to benefit from governmental extraordinary measures, financial breaks from partner corporations, I was still very far from resolving my financial stresses. But with the extraordinary support of Dr. Bak, we made a significant action that would allow me to stay true to myself, my ongoing commitment to improving the future of underprivileged children in my community.

> "Let us use the pandemic recovery to provide a foundation for a safe, healthy, inclusive and more resilient world for all people."
> Antonio Guterres, UN General Secretary

AFTERMATH was only the beginning of this new journey. My new friendship with Dr. Bak and joining **THE ALPHAS** allowed me to connect with other extraordinary individuals who, by now, need no more introduction: Dr. Paul Ouellette, Dr. Anil Gupta, Dr. Paul Dominique, monsieur le maire and dentist, Phillipe Fau, Dr. Nach Daniel, Dr. Julio Reynafarje and so many others. Each and every one of them had a different view and unique perspective to the unprecedented challenges that our industry was facing.

THE INCUBATOR

Summits after summits and meetings, **THE ALPHAS** became the incubator for thoughts, ideas and a great testing laboratory to expose new visions. It is in this context that I humbly propose a solution that could not only rescue our industry by preventing the explosion of costs but also the opportunity to come together as a profession and significantly contribute to the war effort against the devastating consequences of COVID-19.

So with this in mind, Dr Bak baptized it the **LACOSTE INITIATIVE**. I have said it many times before, true experts and institutions should set guidelines and protocols no single individuals.

This is no time for competing; my friend Dr. Bak said it so many times: "All interests aligned" and by that, he literally meant all of the interests of the entire planet. He is right. To this, I added that the planet, our only home, had never been so small and that our common destiny had never been so interconnected. By unifying and thinking collectively, we could come up with excellent solutions.

At this point, ideas and novel approaches were emerging from all kinds of sources. Yet critical facts remained true and could not be overlooked. At the very moment of writing theses lines, it remained unclear whether aerosol producing procedures and the particles they generated had sufficient viral load to cause an infection. Furthermore, as they went, health care systems around the globe were in need of reinforcements.

I have always defined myself as a health care professional who happens to be a periodontist, not the other way around. As such, I have always had a broader view of my profession. Health includes the mouth, the body, and the mind. Furthermore, it includes habits such as exercise, healthy eating and education.

In a very broad sense, a true health care professional has a moral obligation to actively promote all of those parts with the use of knowledge or by referring to other experts.

In light of this context, it appeared clear to me that all initiatives for the reboot of dental practices would need to stand on principles of safety for both staff and patients, maintaining and or improving access to care and contribute to the overall wellbeing of our society.

Simply put, after proper phone screening, patients could come in dental offices and be tested using new technology that allows for fast results. All positive patients would then be sent home with proper referral channels allowing fast track access to critical care as symptoms appear while negative patient could move on to standard care using universal precautions.

This approach could effectively allow dentists to resume their practice, would multiply testing sites and availability, contribute to strategic confinement strategies all while reducing the pressure on health care systems.

Quickly, **THE ALPHAS** went to work and questioned the initiative. After an emergency session, we set out a world summit with leaders of 4 different countries, USA, France, Peru and Canada to address the issue.

What about false negatives? What about cost? What about unaccounted possible risks? In the end, the idea was accepted in principle but we would effectively need more Alphas to join and contribute to work on its limitations.

In essence, that is the true spirit of the Alphas. Egos are checked at the door and we work together to move forward to the greater benefit of our profession and ultimately the world. Humbly, this is a call to all who wish to contribute and to all that believe that the power of us is stronger than the power of self.

By the time of this writing, CANADA just legalized testing of COVID-19 to Dentists. Just like teledentistry, we can never say that we made that happen, but we did influence the table in the right direction, offering our help. Still, this is 2 on 2!

> "We are what we do. Excellence, therefore is not an act but a habit."
> **Aristotle**

As the journey continues, I will humbly contribute to push the boundaries, encourage others to join **THE ALPHAS** and hope to leave no doubt about my relevancy.

This is how we will prevail. This is how we will all survive. This is how we will prosper, as one. This is **RELEVANCY**.

Dr. BAK NGUYEN

CHAPTER 16
"A NEW WORLD DIALOGUE"
by Dr. BAK NGUYEN

Nothing is harder to write a book than to start with your main idea in the first chapter: to build from the difference. After that, I reacted to my own ideas, those of Paul and the events and summits happening in between.

When you open your first chapter will everything that you got, you then have to provoke new things to happen in real life to keep writing. If anything, **COVID-19** proved that the pace of life has changed.

It is quite a paradox, on one hand, we have so much free time within the **GREAT PAUSE**, on the other, things change by the minutes throughout the world and this war. If we want a real chance out of this one, speed is the essence. The speed to understand and to assert, the speed to analyze and to adapt, the speed to re-assert and to adapt again. If there is one thing everyone can agree on is that no one has the answer, at least the perfect answer.

> "In the COVID war, time is not the answer, speed is.
> Speed, humility and flexibility."
> **Dr. Bak Nguyen**

At the beginning of the war, Bill Gates was the forward thinker and philanthropic billionaire who has foreseen this, years in advance. He was a hero along with Elon Musk who put his fortune, ingenuity and power to the war effort. Well, a few weeks later, Musk remains a hero while Gates falls in disgrace, from Savior to Devil.

What caused such drastic changes? Well, even if a vaccine is still is progress, people criticized the proposal of M. Gates to vaccine the world. Even worse, to keep an electronic record of who contracted the virus, who got vaccinated and who isn't.

Fear causes people to change side very quickly.

Although we can each have our own opinion on this matter, it will, sooner rather than later, become a part in our lives. Will there be mandatory vaccination? Will there be an electronic bank of personal data created?

Well, no one can now ignore those questions. Two months ago, this is not even an idea one would entertain in the public place. If the confinement lasts another 2 months, people will be begging for a vaccine. Do you see the speed of change?

"Bigger the pain, bigger the fear, bigger the intolerance."
Dr. Bak Nguyen

And what intolerance are we talking about? The usual casualties of **FEAR** are **FREEDOM** and **INDIVIDUAL RIGHTS**. After this crisis, will we still be free to choose and be the master of our own body? Suddenly, we are all walking the shoes of the women right's movement.

Can power force upon us something we do not want? Isn't that violation, rape? On the other hand, can someone refuse to be vaccinated and cause the next pandemic? Who has the answer?

But wait long enough for the pain to grow big enough, and those questions will much be waived by default. Can anyone today choose not to pass to the security check at an airport?

> "In given time, FEAR will dictate all the answers."
> Dr. Bak Nguyen

Can we agree that the pace and depth of change have taken a new level of significance? In this scenario, can we afford not to have a voice? This is the reason why we must find our relevancy and our voice in the new world order **post-COVID**. And we must do it fast.

Our old ways to structure and organized won't withstand the next wave of change. If we are still waiting for the perfect solution and the 0 risk; well, we might not last to debate its merits.

At the same time, we cannot rush into **FEAR** and paranoia and remove all the rights and progress made to human and civil rights since the last centuries.

> "Too many have sacrificed too much for us to now let FEAR take it all away. Remember the fights of our forefathers and foremothers."
> Dr. Bak Nguyen

Our only chance is to leverage on the **PARADOX OF COVID-19** to find a way out: to use the given time to adapt quickly and to keep readapting. In the **OVERACHIEVERS'** summit, I've been asked how to react as we do not have all the information concerning the pandemic.

Well, my response specifically to the **COVID** crisis was that as the world should act as one, united and we copied one another, reacting to this enemy. We all made the same mistakes and the same protocols. From whom will we learn a better alternative in the case of failure?

What we lost perspective of, looking to standardize, is the diversification of the nations. Imagine if, within the last two months, each country was fighting in their own way to win this war. For as long as the communication and sharing of information are fluid, we might already improve our response and knowledge of this VIRUS. Instead, we put all the eggs of Humankind in the same basket, copying one another.

Are facial shields, masks and Hazmat suits the way to go? Or is it the testing and screening at a large scale? And which test is the most accurate? Which is more affordable? Which is the most reliable? Can a disinfection protocol in a negative air pressured room be the solution as proposed in Hong Kong?

"Since perfection is a lie, perfection is nothing but pride!"
Dr. Bak Nguyen

No one has a clear answer. And that's not the problem, the problem was that we were all looking for the same answer in the same direction. That's the cost of perfection, that's the price we pay for our lack of humility and corroboration.

Science taught us to try and learn. Even mother nature evolves as such. Why are we looking to advance, looking backward? In the name of standardization? I am not, but not at all, criticizing.

I am simply pointing out an inefficient and dangerous way to think and to react, especially at the pace of today's change.

Much more than the rest of the planet, we, the medical, the dental core, we have a heavy tendency to look for perfection and limit our risk to 0. Keep in mind that perfection is pure pride, that perfection will handicap your speed of reaction and even worse, perfection will blindside you of the alternatives and severely handicap your flexibility to readapt.

Is this a conspiracy theory? Not at all, look at how fast the virus is mutating. Our clinical protocols have to also mutate. Can we afford pride and perfection any longer?

We should act as a network and share in real-time our results with each other. If anything, the web has proven how more efficient are hubs distributed all over the globe sharing and connecting, than a single central terminal.

So should we rebuild our society and industry, with hubs distributed all over the planet where one can take over for the other and vice versa? But are we wise enough to accept such change? Or will we surrender to **FEAR** and double down on central power? This isn't a debate, it is an evolution.

Not a revolution either, we do not have such time. The only way to do so is to organize and to participate actively in a solution, an alternative to the solution, a new dialogue. We are not looking to be right anymore, we are looking to keep searching and to keep adapting.

This virus outsmarted us, all of us. And it is mutating. What will be next? Do you think that virus mutated from a central power with standardization and compromise?

Once again, I do not have the solution, but the pain is real and the price we all paid is already too great to keep making the same mistakes again and again. We must build better and wiser, humble and flexible, always ready to keep evolving. Our enemy is not another nation anymore, it is a **VIRUS**. Are we ready to be outsmarted, outpaced and out of breath in the name of pride and perfection?

I didn't think so. As I am a man of solutions, I will use my speed and momentum to lead **THE ALPHAS** to open as many **INITIATIVES** as possible, as diverse as possible, as opposite as possible, for as long as the clear goal is a better collective future. What? I leave to each **ALPHA**.

I will empower to the best of my abilities each **INITIATIVE**. How? We will learn the best practice of each other as we will keep challenging each other to do more and to do better, even the winners.

Who? If you are reading these lines, you know you are one of us. The more we are, the better our chances for success and for better odds to outsmart, outpace, and outgrow the enemy,

THE VIRUS. The time of differentiation is over. That's how we've broken the glass ceiling.

> "Now, we stand together from and with our diversity to face the common enemies, both from within: THE VIRUS and PRIDE."
> Dr. Bak Nguyen

Only by leaving **PRIDE** aside, have we a chance to **HUMILITY**. To stop looking down on our patient telling them what they need is a start. To listen to them with the possibility of rethinking our ways is the next step. And no, our licenses and disguised monopoly won't protect us much longer.

Oh, and by the way, whatever needs protection isn't as strong as we are pretending. Those are the shields of the past. They are the burden of tomorrow and the double price you paid today. We need to open up and to listen, not to shield up and to impose… What we don't even know, if it is still relevant or obsolete?

You want a real application of this? Well, how will you apply **THE OUELLETTE INITIATIVE?** Except for Dr. Ouellette and his sons, no one of us has ever tried that before, on a global scale. Well, I can tell you what I will be doing. I am learning as much as I can from Paul and will address all of my active patients to offer them the break and new social pact.

I will not pretend that I know what I am doing, only that it was the best alternatives to our present crisis and will keep Paul in the loop. But I will also open up to them to include them in the draft of the solution. Whoever has connections, experience, skills to help make it work will be welcomed to join the board of the initiative.

The idea is to get it up and running swiftly and to readjust as many times as needed on the way. And even when it will be up and running smoothly and flawlessly, my deepest hope will be to keep that **DNA** of adjusting and sense of emergency to keep us on our toes; to keep us at our best! That's how we will keep our relevancy, how we will raise our relevancy: being humble, flexible and acting and reacting swiftly.

About the other **INITIATIVES**, I can tell you that if **PAUL DOMINIQUE'S INITIATIVE** is not done within our ranks, it will be done by someone outside of our ranks. You can agree or disagree with his proposal, it won't change the fact that the people have a will and technology, the means. We can choose to be relevant or not, to have a voice or not.

About the **LACOSTE INITIATIVE** to keep our cost of upgrade post-**COVID** low and smart, it is in our interests to push the dialogue and to find all possible alternatives and solutions, so, in given time, we might have a solution to propose or, at least, have the right questions to ask the so-called experts with their proposed solution.

Remember, the collectiveness will always outsmart the smarter amongst us. Since the **VIRUS** does not network, at least, not that we know of, this might be our edge to win this war, our collectiveness.

> "The edges to win this war is our collectiveness and diversity, with humility, sharing and flexibility."
> Dr. Bak Nguyen

This is not just the chance to lead the rebuilding of our profession and industry. It is our chance to lead the reconstruction of the world economy and society to outsmart, outpace and outgrow the **VIRUS**. Remember, both the enemies we are facing are from within, **THE VIRUS** and **PRIDE**.

Networking, even from an ocean away and genuinely share is a mean to care. To keep our humility by involving our peers and those we serve in the dialogue is our leverage to relevancy, not just for its final results, but also from its process.

> "Dialoguing is the first step to relevancy."
> Dr. Bak Nguyen

To forget **PRIDE** and **PERFECTION** to stay flexible will ensure our evolution and ease the transition. To help because we can and not because we care will unleash all of our potential locked inside. To keep adapting and readapting will up pace our evolution and kickstart the new world dialogue, not order. That's relevancy!

> "For a new world dialogue, not a new world order!"
> Dr. Bak Nguyen

This is how we will prevail. This is how we will all survive. This is how we will prosper, as one. This is **RELEVANCY**.

Dr. BAK NGUYEN

CHAPTER 17
"REINVENTING YOURSELF"
by Dr. PAUL OUELLETTE

Ten years ago, in Brevard County Florida, I was in the midst of the **GREAT RECESSION** that started December 2007. February 26, 2010, a Florida Today front page article's headline was "From Bad to Worse". Post-shuttle job outlook darker in light of the president's budget.

There were 50,000, steadily increasing, layoffs in Brevard County by February 2010. Businesses related to the Space Industry were closing and laying off our dental patients. It was a severe financial setback for our family that was as significant, if not more, than the current 2020 Pandemic Depression.

I do not want to be the first to call the current financial event a Depression, as I have never lived in a Depression as severe as the one from 1929 to 1933 plus years. However, I predict today, the 2020 pandemic financial downturn may be called the **COLOSSAL DEPRESSION** as we may be approaching 30% unemployment in the USA in the near future.

As of this writing, America has reached 15% unemployment in just 2 months. We only have another 10% to go to match the **GREAT DEPRESSION**. History is rapidly repeating itself in real-time, but this time it could be worse than the Great Depression. Let's work together and come up with solutions to disprove the worst-case scenario.

The Khan Academy posted on the Internet the following description of the 1929-1933 Depression:

The Great Depression was the worst economic downturn in US history. It began in 1929 and did not abate until the end of the 1930s. The stock market crash of October 1929 signaled the beginning of the Great Depression. By 1933, unemployment was at 25% and more than 5,000 banks had gone out of business.

Brevard County Florida, home of the NASA Kennedy Space Center, was a wonderful place to live and raise our four children. We were truly living the dream in Melbourne Florida. Our one-acre waterfront home complete with tennis court, dock, boats, jet skis and especially great fishing was where we spent most of our leisure time.

Looking back, I wished I had spent more leisure time, but I was building my dental practices. At that time we had eight offices in Central Florida and one in Atlanta, Georgia. We practiced all dental specialities under one roof. Working with General Dentists, Orthodontists, Endodontists, Periodontists, Prosthodontists, and later Implant Dentists was the beginnings of the Interdisciplinary Ouellette Family of Dentists, "Dental Dynasty".

Jonathan and Jason were just finishing their dental school and specialty programs. Life was great! We were all learning new skills from our very talented group of professionals.

We added several hygienists to our team. Florida was just allowing hygienists to administer anesthesia. I immediately sent my hygienists for training and certification. This was great for me, as an orthodontist, because at this time in my practice development, I would not EVER touch an anesthetic syringe.

I always told my family and friends, I just point my finger and direct. It was great to get back into the basics-of-dentistry and re-learn old procedures (like giving shots!) and many new ones. This was the beginning of my **REINVENTION!**

We started a local study club that would meet once or twice a month on Tuesdays. Our favorite food was Sushi. In the beginning, it was just a social club focused on great Japanese food and camaraderie. However, it evolved into a great learning experience for me.

Dr. King Kim, a very talented Oral Maxillofacial Surgeon, was one of the doctors in our study group. He and his partner, Dr. Rick Schmid Oral Surgeon, would corroborate on orthognathic surgical cases. These cases could be classified in the category of *Extreme Makeover Dentistry*.

Dr. David Spector, one of my very first friends in Brevard County, was working for one of the first DSO companies in Florida. He was probably the top, if not one of the best dentists, in their organization. He developed a very successful practice in Melbourne, Florida. David performed beautiful cosmetic dentistry (that was AFFORDABLE) and helped us immensely in creating beautiful smiles in Brevard County. He also was my personal dentist.

It was David that introduced myself and my sons to participate on SIFAT (Servants in Faith and Technology, Birmingham, Alabama) mission trips to Ecuador. He was also instrumental in later helping us develop the **Earn Your Smile program**, which served as basis for what Dr. Bak will be calling **THE OUELLETTE INITIATIVE**. David and his wife Carmen tragically lost their son Eric in a fateful accident in 2007. The Earn Your Smile Program is dedicated to his son Eric Spector.

Our practice, Dental Specialists of Central Florida, was booming prior to the 2008 economic downturn. We had expanded our network of offices to eight locations. Life was good! Not much leisure time, but I was building a network of offices for my sons to take over.

As we slowly dug ourselves out of the **GREAT RECESSION**, I decided to become an Implant Dentist. I told my family and friends: "That's what I want to do when I grow up!" At that time I was in year 38 as an orthodontist. It was my relationships with respected and talented colleagues that started my journey.

Re-inventing myself has never been the end game. My career has had many journeys from building a network of 33 group practice offices and starting a motivational orthodontic supply company Century 2001 that is approaching 40 years in business. We sell our products to orthodontists and local businesses such as the NASA Space Center.

The first journey was becoming an orthodontist. At the early age of 14 years my Orthodontist mentors, Dr. Jarabak and Hilgers helped me complete that journey. With 50 years as a dentist, I am looking forward to more projects, working with my sons and colleagues, definitely not retiring.

One of the most talented dentists in our group practice in 2010 was Dr. Patrick Williams from New Smyrna Beach, Florida. The Space Center closing made the economic downturn even worse for Brevard County and adjacent counties such as Volusia County.

Daytona Beach is located in Volusia County, home of the Daytona International Speedway. I remember commuting to Atlanta from Daytona's airport that is right on the same grounds as the Speedway. I made the mistake of returning from Atlanta just as the 4th of July race ended. It took me more time to get out of the parking lot than the flight from Atlanta.

Dr. Williams had a beautiful boutique dental implant practice in Volusia County. He provided high-end implant dentistry to his patients. When the Space Center closed it was like someone turned off the water spigot. His flow of implant patients dried up seemingly overnight. He visited our office looking for a job as an associate.

We gladly asked Patrick to join our group and help us dig ourselves out of our **BIG DECLINE** in our practices. Dr. Williams possessed that *Special Set of Skills* as an implant surgeon and the prosthetic rehabilitation skills used for very complex cases.

Working with him, I would frequently look over his shoulder taking mental notes and learning from a MASTER. I understood why he was number one in his dental class at University of Florida. It was reported that he only missed one question on his national dental boards. He still thinks he answered it correctly. Thank you Patrick for mentoring me.

In 2010, we discussed taking the Atlanta AAID Maxi Dental Implant 10-month mini-residency that trained general dentists and dental specialists to perform implant dentistry. Dr. Williams could have been one of our instructors as he was already very experienced. He wanted to earn credentials and be able to call himself an Implantologist.

The AAID is one of the first credentialing organizations that certifies dentists in this relatively new specialty. The very first specialty in dentistry was Orthodontics. Implant Dentistry will soon, we hope, be recognized by the CODA certifying branch of the ADA.

Dr. Williams recorded and transcribed every lecture for he and I. He also provided this information for the entire group of 65 residents. He shared his recordings and notes with all of us. His appreciated efforts helped everyone pass the AAID written certification test we took in December 2010 when the mini-residency was completed.

Dr. Williams and I sat for the clinical examination in Chicago held at the ADA Headquarters. We had to present 3 dental implant cases and be tested at 7 stations with two AAID examiners at each table. I was the only orthodontist to sit for the exam. It was scary for me. Thanks to Dr. William's 3 years mentoring, I nailed it!

In 2013, Dr. Williams and I attended the AAID meeting in Phoenix Arizona to received our certificates as AAID certified Associate Fellow Implant Dentists. I REINVENTED myself with Dr William's help!

I continued to learn more and more about this great new field in dentistry. Implant Dentistry has opened more doors than orthodontics. My son Jonathan is called the *Implant Dragon of Orlando*. Look him up on Instagram to see some of his complex cases. Jason is an orthodontist practicing in Jacksonville and St. Augustine.

In closing, I researched the Internet for find information about re-inventing oneself. I was happy to see that I covered most of the points of three or more other authors. Below are some questions to ask yourself when you start your journey to the new you.

Do you really want to change?
Can you prioritize your tasks?
Do you associate with the right people?
Do you enjoy learning new skills?

Will you find a mentor to help you navigate your journey?
Can you be creative and not be afraid to experiment?
Can you be completely honest with yourself?
Will you get out of the box and your comfort zone?

Can you start with baby steps one at a time?
Can you be ready and accept failure on track to the new you?
Can your journey be a new learning experience?
Do you want to stay in the game?

Can you remain positive, even in the face of adversity?
Will you push yourself to your limit?
Would you like to not ever be bored again?
Are you willing to try out new things?
Can you be resilient?
Will you establish a support system?
Do you know your strengths and weaknesses?
Can you find the courage to do things you may not think of doing before your journey?
Can you stay committed to the end of your journey?

Hopefully, you thought about each question and have your plan formulated. I am looking forward to someday meeting the New You!

As our personal journey goes, we need to reinvent ourselves and find the fun doing so. As the relevancy of our kinds, dentists, goes, we most do it while reaching out for one another. This quest is not a personal one, not anymore, not after **COVID-19**.

Now is the time to fast track our own evolution to empower and to fuel the **RELEVANCY** of our profession, using the same principle of reinventing, but this time, for the collectivity and the reaffirmation of our kind. We are dentists!

This is how we will all survive. This is how we will prosper, as one. And then, a colleague and guest author, Dr. Anil Gupta, suggested the following: REINVENTING OURSELVES, not to survive, but to thrive. I agree with him.

This is **RELEVANCY**.

Dr. BAK NGUYEN

PART II
"AN OPEN DIALOGUE"
by Dr. BAK NGUYEN

As the confinement is approaching an end, we are all busy coming back to our practice, our practice and perhaps our life. Is that right? I believe that the answer is a negative one. Our lives have changed forever. Now, the real challenges arise.

Once more, we will be diving into production, efficiency and protocols. What about the standard of care? What about our purpose? What about what the population told us at the light of COVID-19, 3% relevancy?

This is the call, this is our mission, should we choose to accept it. I know, I will. The **GREAT PAUSE** has been an awakening call and I, personally, won't go back to sleep as memory fades the trauma into scar.

I have to say how privilege I feel to have connected and shared with each one of you. Dr. Paul Ouellette, Dr. Eric Lacoste, you have been my closest allies, joining my as ALPHAS since the first day. You have also each co-signed with me a book, Dr. Ouellette, **RELEVANCY** and Dr. Lacoste, **AFTERMATH**. And yes, we've came with the idea, written and completed those within our time in confinement! That's my gene…

I truly believe that our work, our words, will be the opening for a new era, both in our industry and for the economy. Those were the 2 causes I stood up for, forced in confinement: to save our Economy and our Dental Industry.

Well, at the light of the **ALPHAS' JOURNEY**, I can tell you that the **DENTAL INDUSTRY**, if you join me, will lead the way to rebuild a new **ECONOMY**, one stronger, one fairer, one bolder!

Yes, we are a small industry, but we are a noble one. It is time for us to stand up and to lead the way, by example. What we are proposing is a direct answer to the call of the United Nations secretaries for the last 2 decades.

Well, this time, we heard the call and we will lead the way, us, dentists of the world , not only the doctors but all of our team and industry. It is time to leave the medals and divisions behind.

Just like we will need all our team members to rebuild our practice, we will need all of the individuals of our industry and their collective will and intelligence to lead the way into a better future, a better dental profession.

Dr. Anil Gupta, Dr. Paul Dominique, Dr. Nach Daniel you have accepted my invitation, not only to join **THE ALPHAS** but to be guests authors in **RELEVANCY**, the cornerstone of the rebuilding. I thank and welcome your words and thoughts.

Dr. Robert Boyd, Monsieur le maire Dr. Philippe FAU, Dr. Julio Reynafarje, Dr. Eric Pulver, I would love to extend my invitation for you to join as guest authors. Our profession will greatly benefit from your wisdom and mindset for the future.

Yesterday, as I took a few days to gather my thoughts after the **SUMMIT OF THE OVERACHIEVERS**, I finally decided to make a website to feature all of the interviews and summits I led as **ALPHA**. Actually, I was just a man looking for answers when it started, a few weeks ago.

Now, making the profile of each of my mentors accepting my invite, each of my friends joining in and each of those I met on the way, I truly feel the significance of standing amongst **ALPHAS**.

I owe a special thanks to Christian Trudeau and André Châtelain my dear friends and mentors who have accepted to share their thoughts and wisdom with me and with the world. Terry Kilakos, Clint Saraylian, Thierry Lindor, you were the first presidents who generously accepted my call. Thank you for sharing, thank you for believing in the future, in us.

A special thought to Tranie Vo, my wife and business partner who, even if she did not appear in this book, made everything possible, taking care of the company while I was busy, taking care of the **ECONOMY** and our **PROFESSION**. Without her, I will still be drowning in the midst of this crisis' bureaucracy. She gave me the chance to find a strong footing, not only for myself but for all of us.

Anil Gupta, my great friend and international motivational speaker, by kindly accepting my invitation, you brought your status and fame into our initiative. I stand humbled and grateful. Thank you.

Sylvain Guimond, how could I go on without mentioning your name? As you were busy with all your interviews and interventions on TV and radio, you took the time, a Sunday morning to share your thoughts and message of hope with me, with us. Many people use the label friend, you truly give it its meaning.

Being a friend is to take the time. Beside your fame and Anil's, I shy to call myself an **ALPHA**… or I am pushing myself even harder to not fall too far behind. Thank you.

Oh, and what to say to the man who was by my side before and in the crisis, making things possible. He introduced me to the art of podcasting, then we found ways to shot Hollywood grade interviews and masterclass without a crew.

Then, once again, he showed me ZOOM at the beginning of the confinement (which is the basis on which I led all of the interviews and Summits). He didn't stop there, he kept pushing for more, for better.

I today hold the power of a TV Studio, a PRODUCTION CREW, a PODCAST powerhouse within my palm. Coach and strategist, Jonas Diop, my dear friend, thank you for being part of my endeavors.

And then, all of you joined. Dr. Alain Aubé, Dr. Thomas Nguyen, Dr. Agatha Bis, Dr. Mohammad Javaid, Dr. Nail Dia, Dr. Maria Kunstadter, Howard Reis, Mylène Dubois, Jocelyn Grégoire, Martin Lavallée, Christopher Salador, Gregory Excellent, Johnny Mouyanar, Dr. Duc-Minh Lam-Do, Dino Masson to share the hope and to join the vibe. Thank you for each and every one of you.

To honor our journey, yesterday I made a video clip call **THE ALPHAS, AN AMAZING JOURNEY**. Even though I never met many of you in real life, I feel the nostalgia of the end of a great journey. What am I talking about? This isn't the end, merely the beginning! Even as the **GREAT PAUSE** will come to an end, we will continue, we will prevail.

As I edited hours and hours of footage, it hit me how positive we all were, even in the midst of doubt and insecurity. I would like to invite all of you to share your thoughts, once more with me, but this time, in writing. I will like to invite all of you to write a letter of hope, sharing your perspectives and hope toward a better economy and society.

Those writing about **DENTISTRY** will be joining **RELEVANCY**, and those writing about the **ECONOMY** will be joining **AFTERMATH**. This is our legacy, this is our chance. This is History, our history.

> "In times of crisis, one has to reinvent oneself."
> Dr. Bak Nguyen

With humility and gratitude, I thank you for your openness and trust. As I said it many times on air, here's my promise to all of you: for as long as I will be leading **THE ALPHAS**, I do not care if your views and opinions stand opposed to mine, as long as it is about a better collective future and that your line of thoughts can be followed, you'll have the floor, and I will help you.

This is what came known as an **INITIATIVE**. Each Alpha can lead his own initiative and recruit other **ALPHAS** to join. As Dr. Jean De Serres shared: we will build from the differences!

I can't wait to read your thought and to edit them into our books, **RELEVANCY** and **AFTERMATH**. On the note, all profits of **AFTERMATH** are vouched toward philanthropy, the first 100K going straight to support the children of Laval, thanks to Dr. Eric Lacoste's presence. We are also seeking a foreword from the UN secretary of Africa… wish us good luck!

"For a new world dialogue, not a new world order!"
Dr. Bak Nguyen

This is how we will prevail. This is how we will all survive. This is how we will prosper, as one. This is **RELEVANCY**.

Dr. BAK NGUYEN

CHAPTER 19
"THE PACE OF CHANGE"
by Dr. NACH DANIEL

Writing a book or a chapter in a book has always been on my bucket list. I've always told my wife Josée that one day I would like to write a book. A book about my life experiences. A book about my struggles and my successes. A book that would benefit the young and the old.

The pandemic has given me, and to millions of people around the world, the **gift of time**. The time to stop and look around. The time to do the things that we all wanted to do but always postponed.

> "The pandemic has given us and
> our planet time to heal."
> **Dr. Nach Daniel**

I established my practice in Monkton, New Brunswick in 2006. I've dedicated most of my time and energy on perfecting my surgical skills and delivering the highest standard of care. My dedication has pushed me to work countless hours, in the constant pursuit of new innovations and technologies which could improve the standard of care.

My quest led me to believe in the importance of innovation and collaboration for the well-being of both my patients and my practice.

As I became an oral and maxillofacial surgeon, I focussed all of my attention on building a good and sustainable relationship, as well as building the best environment to deliver predictable and constant quality services. This obviously turned out to be a very difficult task.

> "In the competitive world of dentistry, building relationships is not always easy."
> Dr. Nach Daniel

However, within the last 15 years, I was very fortunate to be surrounded by a number of qualified clinicians with the same philosophy. We built and sustained a wonderful relationship, having at heart one purpose: to deliver the best, nothing but the best.

During all this time, I was never proponent on social media and certainly shied away from it, both on the personal and professional side. My Facebook profile sat idle as I always believe that the best and strongest relationships are built through personal encounters.

However, I quickly realized that our world is changing and that socialization and the way to connect have changed drastically over the last few years. As the pandemic lingered, I received the gift of time. I was parked on the bandwagon of webinars and social media in the quest for answers.

My search led me to discover Dr. Bak, a charismatic dentist/entrepreneur from Montreal. While looking at his LinkedIN profile I quickly noticed that he graduated from Dentistry a year after me and from the same University. I instinctively decided to contact Dr. Bak and add him to my circle of new online social friends.

This social media frenzy allowed me to make so many friends in such a short time. I was amazed by how quick and easy it is to connect to so many people. I never thought that this initial contact would develop into a friendship which will lead me to write my first chapter and soon my first book.

Before I could realize what was happening, I was interviewed through teleconference on my perspective of this crisis and my views on the future of our profession. The connection was intense and genuine. In front of a camera, you do not have much place to hide. We openly shared and felt something real.

I've always been a straight shooter, I appreciate efficiency and swiftness. Dr. Bak's style of connecting was one of a kind, one I appreciated.

Believe it or not, Dr. Bak is writing a book every two weeks. A few days after our first interview, he invited me to join as a guest author in his current book, **RELEVANCY**, his 64th. I was both flattered and very intrigued by his methods and mindset. I've always wanted to write a book and I had time! I gladly accepted. That led me to write my first chapter ever.

I was just in for a first step. Soon after, he invited me to join the panel of the **OVERACHIEVERS** at **THE ALPHAS International Dental Summit** to discuss the future of dentistry, the future of our profession. Again, very intrigued, I accepted his invitation. The experience turned out to be very rewarding.

I shared the panel with 4 other overachievers of the industry. It allowed me to better understand the challenges that our dental profession is facing today. Many wonder about the future of our profession. The pandemic has certainly raised many questions.

When will be able to resume our practice? What are the changes that we will have to make in order to kickstart our practices? Will we be able to assume the financial burden of these *improvements*? How will our patients react? One thing remains certain, no one has a clear answer. There are no certainties for the future of our profession.

As I got to know Dr. Bak better, I came to share his concerns on the future of our profession. The idea of relevancy became clearer in my mind as it represented the long-term viability and sustainability of our industry. Paced on the spread of the virus, the speed of change will leave many, many behind. Well, Dr. Bak gave me a taste of the pace of the reaction, and even though, we will have to accelerate if we want to face the challenges ahead.

The COVID-19 pandemic has clearly shown us that even the most robust and stable industries could be paralyzed by a microscopic bug. What will happen to the dental industry in the aftermath of this pandemic? What other types of disruptors will invade our dental space and alter our landscape?

> "Our relevancy has been put to the ultimate test and will have to be re-defined."
> Dr. Nach Daniel

As we get ready to reboot our dental practices, the majority of clinicians are worried about the economic viability of our industry. The new protocols and guidelines which will soon be imposed on us by our respective dental bodies will certainly have an impact on the delivery of care both in terms of cost and accessibility.

How will our industry react? How will we react as clinicians and dental service providers? I truly believe that our future relevancy will depend on our ability to adapt.

> "There is only one way to survive and thrive when faced with circumstances out of control and for which we are unprepared: adapt."
> Charles F Glassman

The last few weeks have given me plenty of time to ponder about the future of Dentistry. It has become clear to me that our survival as a profession and industry will hinder on our ability to instil a sense of collaboration and innovation.

Disruptions in various industries are changing the way we live and interact. Advances in technology and artificial intelligence (AI) are shaping every industry.

> "For those able to adapt, the future looks extremely promising."
> Dr. Nach Daniel

And those who decide to resist, the fast-moving current of technology will sweep them away and they will disappear. How will our industry adapt to change? How will we, clinicians, change our ways and adapt our behaviour to be able to sustain our relevancy?

In the last few weeks, I was able to discuss our relevancy with various leaders of our industry. My discussions have led me to believe that our future and the future of our profession depend greatly on our ability to embrace **collaboration** and **innovation**.

It is difficult to conceive how we will be able to collaborate in today's competitive world. After all, We are all competing for the same patients. Competing for the same treatments and ultimately competing for the same dollar. Each one of us has his own team, competing in the same arena where winning is becoming more difficult and resources are becoming very scarce.

It is slowly becoming evident that our individual efforts to survive and strive cannot stack up against the complex issues facing our industry. It's time for each one of us to acknowledge the importance of collaboration in our efforts to sustain our industry.

In the last few years, we have seen many intruders invade our space and expropriate parts of our expertise. It is time to work together in order to preserve our profession.

> "Coming together is a beginning, staying together is progress, and working together is success."
> Henry Ford

How can we collaborate for the benefit of our profession? Although I don't have a clear answer to that question, I believe that our collaborative efforts have to focus on the sharing of both knowledge and resources.

We have seen a huge effort from various levels of our industry in sharing knowledge. We are all living an overdose of webinars, and although some are geared towards a product or service that the presenter wants to promote, most were designed to share the wisdom and knowledge to improve patient care.

I would like to applaud all those involved in the marathon of webinars and hope that they will pursue their initiative after the pandemic. It is through knowledge sharing that we are able to arm our clinicians with the necessary tools to preserve our relevancy.

Another challenge facing our industry revolves around the cost and scarcity of some of the resources required to practice

Dentistry. The last few years have seen a significant increase in the cost to operate Dental practices.

The advent of new technologies combined with the constant pressure to compete has forced many dentists to invest a significant amount of dollars. These expenses, combined with the rise in employee wages is putting a crunch on our ability to survive. It is also causing a constant increase in the cost of dental treatments and taking a toll on patient accessibility.

I believe that through collaboration and sharing we can significantly reduce the cost of running our dental offices. I see our industry diverging into a cost-sharing model in which we will see a reduction in service points.

A model in which several owners of dental clinics would relocate into a common space and share staff and equipment. This model would allow many clinicians to survive and compete in a market which will certainly be dominated by the giant DSOs.

In 2015, I owned two Oral surgery practices. One in Moncton and one in Fredericton. I was working five days a week and had associates in both locations. I was invested in real estate and involved in many research project with my good friend Dr Sam Abi Nader at McGill University.

It was the time when DSOs were expanding rapidly and spreading their wings across our nation looking for investment opportunities. Their objective was to cherry-pick the best practices and add them to their portfolio. They obviously approached me and inquired about my interest to sell.

I remember my meeting with the CEO of a Dental Corporation. He certainly knew how to maneuver in tight spaces and draw a beautiful portrait of corporate dentistry. However, I was not interested!!! Following my encounter with him, I immediately became reactive and decided to start acquiring dental practices myself.

My instinctive reactivity was not based on monetary gain but on a natural innate response of fight or flight when dealing with a threat or an intruder. I suddenly realized that our dental space was being invaded by Wall Street investors coming to take a bite at our industry and I was not going to standstill.

However, I quickly realized that my decision to start buying practices did not fair well with some of my colleagues and specifically with some of my referrals. "An oral surgeon buying dental practices. He is buying referrals in order to control the market". Ironically, that was not at all my intention.

There were no other oral surgeons in our area in we were the only office dentist can refer to. However, that is how some interpreted it. They suddenly saw me as a threat to their own survival and some stopped referring to me. Overnight, I became a disruptor.

> "It is through disruptions that we are able to innovate."
> Dr. Nach Daniel

Looking back, I do not blame those who jugged me. Their reaction was instinctive. Since, many of those who criticized and alienated me have either sold to me or to other DSOs. The tide continues to shift as more and more dentists reach out to me to inquire about a potential partnership with our group.

East Coast Dental Group has become one of the leading DSOs in Atlantic Canada. Today, my intentions have become much clearer and are not instinctive or reactive anymore. I have gone around full circle and became collaborative as I opened the lines of communications with other DSOs.

Not necessarily for the purpose of selling, but mostly for the purpose of sharing. I have quickly come to realize that we can all grow and succeed much better through sharing. Competition and collaboration are not necessarily exclusive.

> "Competitive collaboration has become the new norm in many industries and Dentistry is not an exception."
> Dr. Nach Daniel

Our relevancy does not only depend on our willingness to collaborate but also on our capacity to innovate and embrace technology. I have always embraced technology and enjoyed the excitement that it brought into my practice.

Every time I invested in a new technology, I felt as if I was a little kid playing with a new toy. The experience filled me with excitement and opened my horizons to new possibilities. I still remember buying my first cone beam scan in 2008. The move quickly shifted my practice and allowed me to become a premium dental implant provider.

I quickly embraced other technologies such as computer-guided surgery and more recently, introduced navigation implant surgery into my office. Every time I introduced a new technology into the office, I could feel a sense of rejuvenation amongst every team member.

However, we should all remember that introducing new technologies should not be confused with introducing a new toy. After all, shiny new toys are expensive and depreciate quickly! Introducing new technologies should always be about improving patient care.

"I have always strived to deliver my patients the best and least invasive solutions."

Dr. Nach Daniel

Let's not all forget that we are living in the knowledge age. We have become consumers of digital and computerized information. Artificial intelligence continues to make way and is reshaping every facet of our lives.

From smart phones to smart lights, to smart cars. Everything around us is becoming "smart" and in some instances, we are losing our ability to think and process information. Is the "smart" at our expense?!

Although AI is becoming an important tool in helping us navigate the narrow streets of our hectic lives and in many ways our dental practices, we should never forget that AI will never replace the human touch. **Empathy** will always be at the core of our most sacred attributes as health care professionals and AI could never replace us.

AI will become our ally in our daily struggles. Therefore, I strongly encourage all members of our profession to embrace technology and welcome it into their practices. **Digital Dentistry** is changing the way we practice by giving us the ability to deliver predictable care. However, many clinicians have not yet adopted it.

Meanwhile, startups and manufacturers have integrated AI into many dental applications in order to streamline our processes and deliver better care. The use of AI in X-ray interpretation is advancing at a rapid pace. Startups such as DENTI AI are leading the way and have demonstrated a significant improvement in the rate of detection of pathologies.

It is becoming clear that these technologies will help us deliver better dental care. AI and machine learning are also opening the way to virtual diagnosis of patients in remote areas without direct access to a dentist.

All these innovations will allow us to reach and help more patients. They will become our allies in strengthening our legacy as the leading health care professionals of the oral cavity and help us re-define our relevance.

This is how we will prevail. This is how we will all survive. This is how we will prosper, as one. This is **RELEVANCY**.

Dr. BAK NGUYEN

CHAPTER 20
"FACING THE FACTS"
by Dr. MARIA KUNSTADTER

As we collectively look at the prospects of going back to our dental office, barriers of resistance both physically and emotionally push us all out of our comfort zones.

Safety for ourselves, our staff and our patients has been taken to an entirely new level. And patients, who were not comfortable about going to the dentist in the first place, have new anxieties about returning for care in this COVID world.

I was delighted to meet Dr. Bak when he invited me to discuss teledentistry. From our interview, he invited me to participate in the First International Summit on TeleDentististry. Being in "the First" summit continues to drive a message of innovation and working with so many amazing innovators that Dr. Bak brought together allows our story to be expanded and implemented.

My successes in the dental profession have always been out of the *comfort zone* of traditional practice, so moving into the post COVID practice of dentistry is just the next phase.

When I started dental school, only 3% of practicing dentists were female. That proved to be a real positive marketing tool for me as patients knew the *lady dentist* and were pleased with the *female touch* in care.

So, my practice growth boomed from the start. We brought the first Yag Laser to the Midwest in 1989 and not only enjoyed using it for the clinical applications but also enjoyed a huge media boom that covered our practice implementing this new technology for patient care.

I opened the first Dental Spa in Kansas City in 2001, I became an early adopter of Invisalign in 2002, and I was appointed the Dental Director for the PAINS Alliance in 2012 as the only dental representative in a national initiative to address chronic pain and that's when I was hit with the perfect storm: **teledentistry**.

When our group joined a conference in Washington, DC in 2013, I kept hearing from the presenters, that dental pain is one of the top 10 reasons people go to emergency rooms. That's crazy! There are no dentists in ERs, and it costs 10X more that care in a dental office. Patients had to wait hours before being seen and were sent away without any treatment or referral for care.

At my conference table were physicians discussing telemedicine and a perfect wave washed over me: "that's what we need!" A virtual dentist in all the *wrong places* people go for dental complaints so they see the right specialist, get the appropriate medications if needed and triaged to a dental office as a referral for care. **The TeleDentists** was born.

Business 101, it all made sense:

1. Market demand - 125M people did not see a dentist last year
2. The ADA said in 2014, $1.7-2.2B healthcare dollars was spent in ERs on toothache codes alone
3. The telemedicine technology had been developed and implemented since 2004
4. We were in the first-place advantage for the market
5. BUT... it took COVID 19 to make teledentistry a household word.

In the last 8 weeks, we have signed contracts with big payor groups to provide teledentistry for their members, have rapidly expanded our MyTeleDentist program to dozens of offices and continue to negotiate with companies in the USA and internationally to provide teledentistry and have had a huge uptick in our direct to consumer site.

People in lock down, panicked about the virus and then developing dental problems need access to a dental professional. Our team consults with the person, make palliative recommendations and can prescribe medications if indicated. Our goal is to appoint that person to a dental office for care if hands-on care is needed.

We have also had a dramatic increase in our program for a dental office to be able to provide teledentistry to their patients. When offices were forced to shut down, that left patients in the middle of treatment and now, more terrified of returning for care.

Shanna Johnson said it best, "Companies that most effectively appeal to consumers in their moments of needs are the ones that come out ahead". Google analytics have shown a 30% increase in clicks on websites with teledentistry. It's an exciting time to be able to bring teledentistry into the dental office.

Who knew that a virtual consultation would be the most personal contact you will have with your patients moving forward in this decade. Gloves off, no shield, no facemask- just you and the patient face to face.

A chance to meet new patients, reconnect with ones that have not been in for a while and our long-time favorites. Virtual visits give dentists the opportunity to meet people where they are *most comfortable* in their homes.

> "It is time for us all to innovate for the success of the future of dentistry."
> **Dr. Maria Kunstadter**

This is how we will prevail. This is how we will all survive. This is how we will prosper, as one. This is **RELEVANCY**.

In times of crisis
It is the perfect opportunity
To reinvent who we are

Dr. BAK NGUYEN

CHAPTER 21
"HATIKVAH"
by Dr. JEREMY KRELL

I was introduced to Dr. Bak Nguyen by Dr. Eric Pulver, an oral surgeon + serial entrepreneur + investor + artificial intelligence evangelist + good friend, in April, 2020. We met by video conference while shelter-in-place rules were in effect in the US and Canada.

Bak, an overachiever himself, was working on multiple projects: bringing the Alphas together on podcasts, two books (or three), and his own innovative care delivery model, Mdex & Co. I introduced myself as a *non-traditional dentist* and what I meant was that I had a combined background in clinical dentistry (DMD), general management (MBA), and entrepreneurship (15+ years proven track record with multiple successful exits). A bit odd for a dentist. Or is it?

Bak and I are collaborating on (at least) a 4-part podcast series that are covering my portfolio of over a dozen ventures at a high level, mostly focused on innovation within the dental industry. We intend to dive deep on each one and even present a problem and solution approach that we think will appeal to dentists who have an appetite for change.

We quickly developed mutual respect as two entrepreneurial dentists. With the Alphas and a well-developed podcast, Bak has the opportunity to speak to a broad audience and highlight the most important lessons learned. What do I bring to the table? Well, you have to continue reading.

The Hope

Hatikvah is a 19th-century Jewish poem and Israel's national anthem. In simple terms, it literally means, "The Hope." It is really about people finding a safe place after a horrific event to drive towards a better future. The kind of hope that lasts forever.

Dentistry is a critical element of systemic health and the healthcare system. Research has shown many links between oral health and overall health. However, it is often glazed over as too small (okay, not that small, according to the ADA's Health Policy Institute, dental spending expected to be USD $140 billion or $390 per person, representing 3.7% of total health spending) and too sluggish to receive the attention that the broader medical sector garners from innovators, investors, and other professions alike.

The COVID crisis brings the additional challenge of controlling for a virus that spreads through aerosolized bodily fluids, which is not new to dentistry (think AIDS in the 1980's).

My hope is that we, as a somewhat self-regulated profession, look deeply introspectively and see the need to change so that we can tackle bigger challenges and stay relevant. I would like to see our profession cut some of the on-the-ground waste. It should not take a dental professional 5+ steps to complete simple tasks end-to-end, think:

Xrays > diagnosing > treating > charting > billing

We need to learn to share ideas and pool resources to solve some of these complex problems (not hold them back due to fear of litigation or copy cats).

> "It takes courage to pursue an idea or a new business endeavor, but this is how we make advancements, and we can do it together."
> Dr. Jeremy Krell

Like Hatikvah, the hope is that we return to our core skills as dentists (doctor + artist + engineer), restore our profession, and reclaim it as one of the **most forward-thinking** medical professions.

The Tools

Restoring and rebuilding require some necessary tools. As our primary goal is the clinical health of our patients, sometimes we need tools ready to use off the shelf.

In recent years, there has not been a shortage of new products or services surfacing in the dental market. The biggest challenge has been how to implement these tools efficiently, making sure that they are seamlessly integrated into a practice's workflows.

In layman's terms, the right hand needs to be able to speak to the left hand. Each step in the process should include a smooth transition to the next step. How many of those exist in dentistry today?

> "When using a properly designed product, the "right" thing should also be the easiest for the user to do."
> Dr. Jeremy Krell

Think: the way doors that you pull versus push are designed. I have spent the past several years building a web of interconnected tools in the growth areas of dentistry. There are many, but some include tech, dental services, consumer brands, and payments. The intention is to be able to ping the nexus from anywhere on the web I have built and leverage the tools in a scalable manner.

For reference, my dental portfolio includes:

- **QUIP**, an oral health e-commerce subscription service)
- **Supply Clinic**, an online marketplace for dental supplies with transparent pricing from authorized sellers
- **Simplifeye**, a virtual practice in a box - 24/7 live chat, scheduling, telehealth, payments
- **Denti.AI**, a radiographic diagnostic assistance and compliance platform
- **Floss Bar**, a mobile dentistry and COVID testing
- **PatientPlus**, a specialist referral and OTC product platform leveraging treatment plans
- **Asprodental**, a modern customizable practice management system with marketing services
- **Verena Solutions**, a contract design and SimpleCap manufacturer

I want to highlight and zoom into **Verena Solutions** and its contract design service. This is a tool for entrepreneurial dentists to work with other engineering expertise and pursue their ideas. One of the most challenging and vulnerable positions to be in is figuring out where and when to start.

As clearly stated on the website, "whether you have an initial design, idea, or patented work, **Verena Solutions** can help you get through a working prototype and into the manufacturing and licensing stage." **Verena Solutions** provides a starting point.

Verena Solutions can work with ideas as early as in your head or the back of the napkin and turn them into professional renders, with manufacturability in mind. The daunting "chicken or the egg" of funding and prototyping can be simplified by working with Verena Solutions.

The manufacturing process can be arduous - time-intensive and expensive, but Verena Solutions has the expertise in mechanical and electronics manufacturing as well as automation (this is how the SimpleCap is produced). Once there is a more mature product conceived, you need to think about distribution, marketing, sales, licensing, and private labeling. Verena Solutions has 25+ years of experience on the business side.

If you have an idea on the back burner and have been waiting for the right time to pursue it, look no more - in one click of a button, you can submit a project to Verena Solutions.

As Dr. Bak often said, "In time of crisis, it is the best time to reinvent ourselves." Well, this will ease your uphill journey to reinvent yourself. Actually, this is how I can sold to the idea to join **RELEVANCY** by Bak.

Evolution

Emerging from the COVID crisis, things will need to evolve and we will need to reinvent ourselves and our practices. Things are not the same anymore. Practices have been in hibernation for months and have furloughed or laid off staff.

They face new regulations and requirements. Patients don't just fear going to the dentist due to pain and cost, now, they fear for their safety. Dental staff now face an additional danger in doing their jobs.

In order to solve these complex problems, we need to share ideas. This will happen on a national basis (think our leaders at professional associations), through smaller engaged populations (think podcasts and influencers), and on an individual basis.

> "We cannot afford to think about competing with the practice across the street anymore."
> Dr. Jeremy Krell

If you have a good idea about how to operate in this new world, you should share it. We are all dentists and, needless to say, our profession needs a push forward, a big one.

There are many tools available, but how you string them together into an operational workflow in your practice is important (think ingredients for a recipe versus the recipe itself).

Practices do certainly vary, but chances are that you are facing the same challenges as others, so if you have found something that works, you should share it.

> "Don't be afraid to try new tools. Don't be afraid to get rid of the old. Don't be afraid to fail."
> Dr. Jeremy Krell

This is how we will prevail. This is how we will all survive. This is how we will prosper, as one. This is **RELEVANCY**.

Dr. BAK NGUYEN

CHAPTER 22
"THE IMPORTANCE OF BEING A GAME-CHANGER"
by Dr. JULIO CESAR REYNAFARJE REYNA

WHY WE CHOSE DENTISTRY

Vocation of service, every person who thinks about helping another without thinking about himself shows his predisposition for this medical career.

My father was an endodontist and one of the founders of the speciality society in Peru. I've always been amazed of the patient's reactions once they have their health problems solved. I learned looking at my father, that a smile is the best of rewards.

That kind of transformation in people is the best incentive to continue working and help more people. The way they treated him, their love for my father were indelible marks that remains in me as his legacy and teaching.

> "Dentistry is a confluence of many disciplines and philosophies."
> Dr. Julio Cesar Reynafarje

To be a dentist, you need a lot of studies, many hours of reading, to learn to research, to develop criteria and strategies. You need to start generating new skills with your hands, from learning how to properly mix 2 materials to sculpting a tooth from a piece of wax with the detail of naturalness.

So, if it requires so much effort, why do we choose dentistry? Simply for the sake of helping, of being better a person. I read an interview of Mother Theresa of Calcutta a couple of days ago, she was asked about how to help people and replied: you still have many years of work left, you only have to do one good thing for someone every day. Soon you will realize that in a while, you will have helped many people. That is the essence of dentistry: doing good things every day.

In the end, we came to a very simple conclusion, dentistry is a person's passion to give, to grow helping and healing people to improve as one.

GROWING UP AS A DENTIST

Dental schools are the beginning of an interesting and incredible journey, it is an element of change, a change in the way of thinking and acting of a person. It takes a common person and prepares them to be a social reference.

The change occurs in several areas. Definitely, knowledge is the first, the more information, the greater the number of possibilities for a solution. Knowledge in itself generates more curiosity, and makes us constantly want to know more, this is the engine that moves a person towards evolution.

Along with knowledge, there is another element that evolves. This is called **criteria**. Criteria is a part of the reasoning, the ability of a person to be able to choose according to logical elements the best option to solve a problem. Summarizing two concepts in a single action, the acquisition of knowledge provides the fundamental elements of logic for the person to make a choice in solving a problem.

The training in Dentistry is not only theoretical, the practical component is a big part of it, the correct handling of materials and technology is fundamental, but the precision, dedication and art in the manual work of the dentist is the success of his treatments and the final solution to the patient's problem.

These elements are carried out in the professional academic training. All this has a factor that links everything learned together, and it is human kindness. It is the way of caring for a patient, it is the power to understand what that person feels, and understand that every disease process also involves an important **psychological factor**.

Being a dentist also means providing personal support to the patient. But, who is responsible for teaching this subject? To all amongst us who are teachers, we must understand that all teachers are mentors and have this role forever.

> "All teachers are mentors."
> Dr. Julio Cesar Reynafarje

After finishing school, we all should have a continuous training process, inside and outside of the office. The dentist must always be updated, the evolution of knowledge is constant. New techniques and procedures are studied and adopted every day.

In the last years, the gap between the early adopters and the conventional dentists has been shorter. Technological improvements enhance our precision and ease our path to perfection and predictability. It not only helps us in the daily work, It also improves the quality of it.

Finally, The strength of dental training is found in the delicate balance between knowledge, criteria, art, technology and human values.

SUCCESS

Success is a word with a very broad and deep meaning. Although it is understood as a good ending or a positive result, I think it holds a deeper meaning.

Success is not measured by endings, success is a process, a growth process, the actual measurement is based on the average of an entire evolution curve, as a natural process, it has ups and downs. We must understand that it is impossible to measure how high something is when the lowest is unknown.

> " Success is a set of measures to achieve an objective with positive results."
> Dr. Julio Cesar Reynafarje

In dentistry as in life, there is no constant, everything is changing. Science is changing every day also, with so many variables between doctors and patients. Evolution and improvement are forever.

A few years ago I decided to improve my work in restorative dentistry with the use of a microscope, learning to use it and adapt it to my way of working was a challenge. Little by little, it became a fundamental tool in my practice.

It is important to say that the process allowed me to also see procedures that were successful for me at the time, but under this new parameter they were not so successful.

In many cases, I wanted to call the patients back to redo what I had previously done. What I mean by this, is that everything is subjective, we can always improve, we must accept the facts with humility and have the will to always improve, for our patients, with the desire to always do the best we can for them.

THE PROBLEM AND THE CRISIS

Every time I review the literature and the advances that are made day by day in our profession, I find the same thing:

> "Simple things become complex,
> and once complexed, they become problems."
> Dr. Julio Cesar Reynafarje

Reviewing some old books, I found an anonymous Chinese thought, which said:

> When you are a child, trees are trees and stars are stars. When we are adults, trees stop being trees and stars stop being stars. When we are old, trees come back to be trees and stars become stars again.

The procedures in dentistry must be simple. They must be performed by recently graduated dentists and those who are already at the end of their career with good results. The job of those who teach is to make a space where the new and the old merge into procedures that are friendly to everyone, SIMPLE.

To name an example, a few days ago I was talking to one of my students in the speciality clinics and she told me: "Doctor, I don't know how to choose between two restoration techniques in the posteriors." Her confusion grew even more when she did a little research on the web, there were studies that spoke well of both procedures and others did not. The question is always the same, what can I do?

My answer was the following: "The resolution of problems in Dentistry should be **Simple**, and you have to choose the one that you think is the best for that patient and can be performed in the best way with your own experience.

The best comparison to this episode I can find is the building of skyscrapers. In the construction of a tower, bricks are used, also cement. We must understand that the choice of our bricks will make a good base, but without a good cement everything falls apart. The Contribution of the builder is the knowledge to choose materials and planning criteria to do a good job.

If you replace the bricks by your dental materials and the cement by your skills and ability, you will find that the difference between your tower to another one is the judgment and preparation you put in, as the builder.

> "If you add a little bit more dedication, your tower then becomes a work of art."
> Dr. Julio Cesar Reynafarje

This *out of the box* thinking is important. Knowing and applying these few concepts will serve you well to find and create solutions, especially in times of a crisis. After two intense weeks of presentations of new procedures and technologies made by doctors all over the world and in consensus with many of them, I summarize what I learned in 4 main points:

> Protecting and solving the patient's problem is the dentist's main mission. Before approaching them, we must take all the possible care methods to do it.

Despite all the advances in the fields of Rehabilitation and implantology, it has not been possible to mimic completely the Natural function, factors such as proprioception and parafunctions continue to generate variables that cannot have a standard. Dentistry should continue to be the **most conservative as possible**.

The digital trend is more and more innovative every day, leading us to perform some procedures in a simpler and more friendly way for the patient and the professional.

Manual lab and clinical work should never be completely replaced by a digital system, digital systems are elemental to make our procedures simpler and precise but they do not replace the diagnosis, professional judgment and criteria to add natural details. Making a parallel to this point, it reminds me of a car factory: many production lines are entirely digitized, but to this day, the finest cars are still handmade.

In summary, problems and a crisis always generate new trends in knowledge and better methodology criteria for the resolution of them.

HOW CAN WE HELP OUR PROFESSION AND SOCIETY

Being able to help is something inherent to the health professional. It is not a complicated task, but in my opinion, we must start from a common point, and it is called **understanding**.

We must understand first of all, who we are going to help, the way they think, how their stomatognathic system works. How it looks when it is healthy, and then, we can recognize what is not working or does not look good. Understand why we are going to restore and what we are going to use to do it to successfully reach the health parameter that we have visualized for that patient.

A few days ago, I talked with my friend, Dr. Bak Nguyen, about the moments we are living right now and how COVID-19 or SARS-CoV-2 are developing around the world. It led me to think and redirect the way in which the dental profession is going to move on and come to the conclusion that we all have to contribute with something that improves our society and in the benefit of our patients.

This disease has not only exposed how vulnerable we can be, it takes lives, destroys economies and paralyzes countries. It has also united families, has made us supportive, and many heroes have emerged to fight every day and night in hospitals. Some of them are caring out their duties in the streets, and others help with their jobs so that together we can get ahead.

Today we have to look forward, we must work together. Dentistry is not an independent profession, it is a medical profession that diagnoses and treats diseases of one of the primary ways of relating between the environment and the person. This is the reason why we have to work in a multidisciplinary way with medical specialities such as gastroenterology, pneumology and infectiology.

Today the dentist has to rethink his office work. I listened carefully to John Nosta. Every day, he constantly updates us regarding this pandemic, following his example of studying and disseminating, I will list the measures that we should take:

Look for improvements in the Diagnosis. The dental history records should be more exhaustive, it should alert us about medical conditions and it should be included in the patient's medical history for future references. The development of AI (Artificial Intelligence) is going to help us a lot with this, it is already doing so. I fully agree with Jan Berger and Mathias Goyen that this helps our patients.

The Academic Update. The dentist must take continuing education courses in the diagnosis of systemic diseases.

Clinical sterilization systems and protocols must be optimized.

The dentist must be **part of the primary medical diagnostic** teams.

Now, on a Patient's point of view.

Personalized Monitoring. The dentist must always be available to attend to the patient, always giving them security and tranquility.

Incorporation of Telehealth or Teledentistry systems. These platforms should have complementary medical consultations. If you are interested you can review the regulations on the ADA page, and include some hours to attend this way in your schedule.

Personalized and documented patient information material. It should be disseminated through the dentist own network.

Well, I hope these suggestions help you, together we can help more people, be a game-changer, and continue working for a better world.

This is how we will prevail. This is how we will all survive. This is how we will prosper, as one. This is **RELEVANCY**.

In times of crisis,
it is the perfect opportunity
to reinvent who we are.

Dr. BAK NGUYEN

CHAPTER 23
"LIGHTNING BOLT"
by ALIA ALAOUI

My husband James and I pulled into the driveway; a magnificent Bellagio-Esque fountain welcomed our black SUV; we had arrived. "Welcome! We're so happy to see you!" - the voices of long-missed friends, Dr. Bak and Tranie Vo.

The quarantine, or "The Great Pause" had put all our lives into a stasis we'd not lived since we were children. Imagine, being at home, you're four years old, and your mother brings you to the paint store. As you sit in the waiting room, you're watching her go through the catalogue, one after the other, with zeal, enthusiasm and passion, excited to pick the new color that would define her new kitchen.

Minutes become hours, hours feel like days, and before you know it, you've spent the entire afternoon, without any source of entertainment, no smartphone, or Nintendo to focus on, and you forgot your favourite book at home. You are sitting, patiently, staring at the showroom clock, watching the minute hands tick, ever so slowly; being a child, our perspective of time is skewed, and we are quickly drowned by boredom as we feel it has been an eternity.

That is what the Great Pause has felt like.

A gathering, a reunion, a reminder of what friendship, comradery, and good times felt like. Within minutes of the soiree, we were whisked away from the pandemic, and all thoughts, concerns and fears of what lies on the outside, evaporated. We were back to the way it was, the way we all so desperately wanted it to be.

We dined on Dr. Bak and Tranie's divine rice noodle and chicken BBQ cuisine. We celebrated with a bottle of Pear Cognac, and drank to friendship and happier times.

As the evening went on, a flood of ideas, thoughts and creativity erupted onto the patio table. Topics ranging from the housing crisis, Personal Protective Equipment, to how can we use our resources to tackle industries plagued by the pandemic.

"You should write a Chapter with us. Dentists from all around the world will be involved". said Dr. Bak. We talked for hours about how the Dental Industry needs change; how the COVID-19 Pandemic has brought forced change, and that dentists are suffering.

How will the New World be? What will it look like? How will patients interact with their dentist? With each passing hour, it would seem we had an answer to each question, only to be followed up with three or four new questions.

How would the Dental Industry need to change? This was the root thought, running through my brain, thousands of neurons firing, stimulating the dialogue.

Like Alan Turing was decoding the enigma machine in World War II, so too was my mind running through endless simulations and likelihoods of success, for what the Dental industry needs to do in order to grow from this crisis.

This is War. An invisible war that blanketed the planet as quick as the evening sun, forcing our society into a provoked state of evolution. There have been horrific casualties, but from adversity, comes feats of technological brilliance; like any creature backed into a corner, it will claw, slash and bite its way through, to survive.

This War is forcing industries to evolve; and just like that, a lightning bolt of thought, as if launched by Zeus himself, presented the single answer to the gargantuan question: How would the Dental Industry need to change? It must evolve.
Agreeing to write this chapter with the colleagues of Dr. Bak, as well as singular topical focus on how to provide value to this book titled **Relevancy,** made writing this, that much more important.

How does the Dental Industry evolve from here? Allow me to provide a thought-provoking concept, take a minute, digest the idea, then continue reading. What if you never had to spend another dollar to attract a new patient again?

You read right! How about never have to ever spend a dime on marketing again? Will that be a great new start? Trimming your business costs is the basic need of any practice; at this point, the "Great Pause" has ravaged societies, banks, and businesses; however, this is an old technique.

What if there was a new way to leverage technology, to not only find patients but bring them to your practice without you having to go and get them? What if the patients, raised their hands, and screamed "I have a toothache! I need a Dentist!" - wouldn't that be a game-changer?

What if an Artificial Intelligence Marketplace could take all the heavy lifting of patient acquisition away, and focus on bringing people and practices together, quicker, and more efficiently than we could ever accomplish before?

The pandemic has forced us to think differently, and with that, some industries who were the Titans of our consumer-driven universe, are nose-diving out of the sky crashing into the ocean with little hope for recovery. Meanwhile, there are other industries that are emerging as thought-leaders, driving innovation and while once could be considered laggards are now the new early adopters to technology.

Dentistry must evolve - embracing technology for business operations, patient acquisition, and marketing needs, is what will enable dentists to focus more closely on patients, and remain relevant in this new societal change.

If we examine the needs of consumers for a second, we know that the Great Pause has forced many to re-evaluate their living situation, personal expenses, health needs, and they have been given a new perspective on what truly is a "Want" compared to an absolute "Need".

We are moving at blazing speeds into a world where the Needs of the consumer will be quickly identified, predicted and driven with an immediate solution.

The more we can predict, and identify those needs, the more relevant, and accurate our treatments will be to the patient. To be relevant, it's about finding the balance between accuracy, needs and capacity; this is where the world of Dentistry needs to be. The Great Pause is not just about a mandatory metamorphosis, it's about survival, and learning to live with the new tools and resources that are birthed from this era of stasis.

Artificial Intelligence can be and should be the tool emphasized that can not only identify the needs of patients but place them with the dental practices that can humbly serve these people.

Teledentistry is quickly gaining steam as one of the predominant contactless patient consultation portals, allowing a direct connection to be made between someone who is in a relevant need for a dental consultation and a dentist who can help. To properly shed the cocoon of the "old ways" in business practices, the adoption of technology can't end with Teledentistry, it is just the beginning.

Leveraging algorithms, machine learning and cluster analysis, Artificial Intelligence can also dominate the digital landscape by finding new patients who have an immediate need, and bring them to a point of consultation within a few moments. This not only reduces the friction of patient acquisition, but it drops the cost-per-patient astronomically as its ability to scale is limitless.

As I took another sip from the Pear and Lime Cognac, we all sat back in our seats, looked up at the stars, and marvelled, for we realized that in that evening we were shaping the future of the Dental Industry.

I took Bak's offer of writing a chapter, because this is bigger than me, and it needs to be said. The Dental Industry is in its infancy stages of the evolution process, but there is no doubt that it is evolving, out of survival.

We began to conclude the evening; we felt we were on to something special. The brilliance of a roaring fire begins with a single spark, and that night, as if Prometheus himself provided the kindling, was the ember that stoked the flame for this chapter.

The Dental Industry has a unique opportunity; to reinvent itself, in every aspect, and part of my contribution is to further the discussion, about leveraging technology, artificial intelligence, and relevancy for customer acquisition, so that the costs to acquire patients drop astronomically, and dentists can focus on the smiles, with peace of mind that they will survive in this new era post-The Great Pause.

As we said our goodbyes and got into our SUV, we drove away, the cockpit teaming with ideas, thoughts, musings, and while driving down the highway, it became all the more clear, this chapter must be written, if for nothing else, than to simply convey a message.

You will Evolve. You will survive. And I will be there to assist and empower.

This is how we will prevail. This is how we will all survive. This is how we will prosper, as one. This is **RELEVANCY**.

Dr. BAK NGUYEN

CHAPTER 24
"THE OPPORTUNITY TO REGROUP"
by MARTIN LAVALLÉE, BAA, MBA

Not long ago, some of you may have thought: "I am too busy, I don't have the time to think, I lack the time to focus, I am simply not taking any time for myself. This pandemic hasn't helped either! Between keeping your business afloat, keeping your family safe and keeping an eye on your finances, you have much on your plate.

Nonetheless, this crisis had brought its loads of interests and opportunities. The opportunity to come together and stand united as a society, as peers. Yes, this crisis too shall pass. We will be resuming our lives, jobs and businesses. And we will have to be ready to face what will be following.

The next few weeks will be of the uttermost importance. It will be the perfect opportunity to review and revise those new ideas that could make a difference in your clinics, the ideas that will push your team forward.

The new reality is that people have suffered financial losses, this added with the general anxiety about a second wave of this virus will keep many people from running back in your dental chairs for both financial and infectious concerns. And this too shall pass!

As an entrepreneur, all that we can do is to stay ahead and being proactive. The options are multiple: to wait and follow the general trend, to seize the opportunity to invest and gain market shares? Maybe, but at what cost? To start a price war on discounted dentistry? With the increases in operational cost, this tactic can surely be challenged on its merits.

Why not take this opportunity to invest in your best assets, yourself and your team? You have been given the gift of time, finally! Why not embrace this given time to rethink your practice, your enterprise, your life? Dentistry will be awaiting your return!

People will be waiting, but it will be up to you to find a way to repackage and to present it in a way that the public will welcome your offer. You know the recipe, satisfied patients will spread their satisfaction through word-of-mouth and, before you know it, you will be busy again.

Listen to your patients, talk to them, reassure them. That's the only way to build and strengthen the trust and unique bond between you and those you treat. The patient's experience and satisfaction, now more than ever, will be a key foundation for your success.

Isn't it the time to rethink your patient's experience? What are you offering? What plus value are you bringing on the table? More than ever, the public will be looking for the best offer, the best experience, the safest environment. There won't be any room for mistake and improvisation. To achieve such results under these unique circumstances is through a great team effort.

It is time for you to revisit your ways and systems, to renew your vision and to look on ways to move forward. This is the opportunity that I urge you to take advantage of, the given time to plan.

I lead an **INTERNATIONAL DENTAL INSTITUTION (IDI)**, I am well aware of the unique challenges ahead. My team and I can support you. You can find support from your peers. You can find support from your team, or you can find support from all of us! Reach out and look for that support. Give it.

Together, we can plan ahead for efficient protocols and a successful comeback from this pandemic. Education and support can help you plan your success, even through such difficult times.

This is how we will prevail. This is how we will all survive. This is how we will prosper, as one. This is **RELEVANCY**.

Dr. BAK NGUYEN

CHAPTER 25
"I AM A FIXER"
by Dr. AGATHA BIS

> "If you do what you've always done,
> you'll get what you've always gotten."
> **Tony Robbins**

I met Bak in the midst of the hurricane we call COVID-19, our generation's pandemic. Most humans live around 80 years so this feels like the world has turned upside down.

But if humans lived a thousand years, this would be the sixth or seventh pandemic that we would facing in our lives. We would then know that it would be difficult, and then we would know that eventually, it would be over. Most importantly, we would know how to prepare for it.

Logically, of course, that makes sense, but emotionally, we are experiencing one or more of many emotions, like being overwhelm, anxiety, stress, depression, helplessness, fear, despair, grief, anger…

But in the midst of that hurricane, as everyone else around me was feeling all those negative emotions, Bak came at me with excitement and passion! He came out of nowhere, literally fell out of the sky (or the cloud, or well, let's face it, through the use of technology) and told me he was inherently "lazy" as I browsed through his endless number of books he has written in the last short while and the amount of people he has positively influenced in the recent past.

The funny thing is that I was drawn to Bak instantly, for reasons that weren't inherently obvious at the beginning. I thought about the fact that he was interesting to talk to. Then it was his ability to use various aspects of technology to connect with people. And then it was his positive, obsessive drive to raise our profession, dentist by dentist, human by human.

After speaking with Bak a few times, it became clear; why I really wanted to connect further, join forces, and be part of Bak's group of influencers… well, it's because I was obsessed with fixing things.

Let me start at the beginning. I wasn't born in Canada. I came through a refugee camp and landed on Canada's doorstep (Pearson International Airport) on my 13th birthday. It was 1982. My parents had no money, did not speak English, and had no clue as to what to do next.

As time went by, and I watched my mom crying from pain after working on an assembly line day after day, and my father becoming more silent as his mind went to work on what to do next, something began to develop inside me. Not sure now if it was rage, fear, overwhelming or simply a lack of understanding, but it grew and evolved into something internal that I call **"the Fixer"**.

My father is stubborn and smart, and that combination served him, and us, very well. His drive to rise above, to achieve more, to build something great, and to persevere, became my drive. His passion to take care of us and provide above and beyond, became my passion. His internal pattern of thinking and processing information became my pattern.

> "I became obsessed with "fixing" things.
> Making things better, perform better,
> do better, feel better!"
> **Dr. Agatha Bis**

I would look at anything in front of me, whether it was math homework, or a friend struggling with a problem, and my mind was possessed with fixing it and making it better. Math homework, check. Friend's dilemma, check. Get into medical school and dental school, check. Build a dental practice, check. Build a better dental practice, check. Build better systems in my practice so we grow exponentially, check.

I fixed and fixed and fixed, and created systems for everything, then improved the systems, and made them even better. There is a calm in that. I find that I can relax when I have everything around me ticking away just as it should.

> "That feeling like you are constantly improving,
> I find that calming."
> Dr. Agatha Bis

And then the unimaginable happens. Some silly little virus shuts the entire world down. We are help prisoners in our homes, without knowing what our sentence will be. Not only do we not know the length of our sentence, but we don't know the conditions we will be confined to as we serve it out.

That is incomprehensible for a "fixer". And yes, just like you, I went through different phases and different emotions trying to cope and understand and get through this pandemic.

I don't do well in "overwhelm" or "sadness" or "helplessness" and that combined with my ADHD, is a recipe for disaster. So I got angry. And anger fuels me. Anger is my best friend at times because it gives me resolve to get my butt off the misery-train and get to work… get to work on "fixing it". But how do you fix a pandemic? How do you fix anything that's out of your control? You get to work on the things you CAN control!

So I pulled out my giant post-its. Yes, I use these big post-its I stick all over my walls, doors, fridge, and start mapping out a new system. What it will be like to go back in a different way.

How can I make it better? How can I make it so I love going to work? What did I not like about the way I worked before that I kind of ignored or got used to?

As I scribbled and scribbled, a new idea formed. A new way of working was born. And as the excitement built, in the middle of the hurricane, I got a message from this guy named Dr. Bak Nguyen, who wanted to have a conversation about the future of dentistry. So when others were watching Netflix, having ZOOM wine parties or eating endless bags of chips and wallowing in misery, we started to discuss ideas and changes that would influence our entire profession to rise above.

So as I write this, I am deeply moved by where this is going. I am beyond excited about being part of **the ALPHAS**, and feel like I am on the right train, moving in the right direction. So let me give you a bit of insight into where my post-its are going and of course, as my involvement with Bak and his group of Influencers grows, I will keep sharing these ideas with all of you so that our entire profession can constantly improve, and gain the respect we all deserve.

Here is a simple idea that came out of my initial **post-it exercise**:

I want you to close your eyes… well, read the next part before you close your eyes because if you close them now, you won't be able to see what the exercise is…

Imagine if you could only do the things you want and eliminate the things you don't want. Start with that. Imagine if, when you came to work, walked into your dental practice, you could step into your op and go straight to the type of clinical work you love to do and strongly believe in.

Imagine if that work was already paid for and scheduled so that when you walked in, your patient didn't question, for the 17th time, what it is you are "planning on doing today" or if their "insurance would cover it".

Imagine your team, your people, your staff, doing what you want them to do, in a way you want it done, without having to stand over them or nag or complain or remind.

As I stood there in a haze of my own imagination, an idea swelled in my mind and took over my consciousness. There was no voice telling me it couldn't be done. There was no person next to me saying "our patients won't go for that". And there was nothing preventing me from writing it down as if it had already happened.

In that mindset, in that frame of contemplation, my father's drive stepped up within me to spell it all out on paper: the system that was going to be the new way of doing dentistry. The new way of running and growing my practice. The new way I would be seen by my patients. And as I build this out and share it with Dr. Bak and **the ALPHAS** and the people that want to listen and learn and share.

> "I am excited about the future, all of our future,
> if we allow it to be different than it was before."
> Dr. Agatha Bis

And in order to do that, we have to adapt, we have to change. We have to shift our mindset from what we lost to what we will gain. We have to allow ourselves to do different things in order to get different outcomes.

So if you get one thing from this, make it this: change one thing, or one idea, or one system. Do one thing different in order to achieve different results. And see where that takes you moving forward.

This is how we will prevail. This is how we will all survive. This is how we will prosper, as one. This is **RELEVANCY**.

Dr. BAK NGUYEN

CHAPTER 26
"I AM DENTIST"
by Dr. DUC-MINH DO-LAM

For the past 16 years, I have been fortunate to practice a profession I cherish, a profession I respect, a profession that has helped shape me to be the person I am today. I owe so much to dentistry.

But dentistry, along with many other industries, will never be the same anymore. Just like the "universal precautions" that were brought upon us forty years ago, COVID-19 brought its load of uncertainties and questions with regards to the way we practice moving forward.

Whether it is because of science and research, or the perception of the public, new standards in dentistry will emerge. In fact, they already did. We see it in many countries whose dentists have reopened their office to see patients on a regular basis.

New HEPA air filtration system, pre-appointment screening process, temperature reading at check-in, personal protective equipment management, daily staff screening log, to name a few, all of those measures are taken to ensure safety and confidence so we can focus on what we love to do most: dentistry.

For the past six weeks, even though I have not been going much to the clinic to see patients, I feel more involved than ever in my profession. Even though our Prime Minister held daily press conferences to update us on the situation, even though we received daily emails from our professional associations, even though a generalized state of confusion and almost despair took over the population, one thing was for sure: oral health does not know that a pandemic hit us.

So how are we, as dentists, as professionals who are there to serve our community, as leaders in the health field, how are we going to maintain that essential service if we cannot operate like we used to? Are we to redefine ourselves? How are we going to reach patients in pain, in the acute phase of dental infection?

Hospitals health care workers are already so overwhelmed and overworked, the last thing they need is to see a dental patient that can be managed in an outpatient setting.

So how do we extend our help to those in need if they are stuck at home, confined or quarantined? One of the aspects of my work that I feel so privileged to have, is that contact we have with our patients who trust us with their oral care. I never take that for granted and believe I have to earn that confidence in every single interaction.

"I have to earn that confidence in every single interaction."
Dr. Duc-Minh Lam-Do

So why not leverage what is already so present in people's everyday life and use it to meet them, be in front of them? If virtual care in medicine has been present for some years now, is there a way to fast-track dentistry here in this space? What if we can adapt to the reasons of the people seeking dental care? What if we can remediate to certain common oral and dental issues without the patient needing to be physically present at the clinic?

Alongside Marco Celli, who engineered the platform, and Dr. Alexis Thériault, MD who specializes in AI applications in medicine, teledentistes.com was then born on those premises: a virtual dentistry interface for consultations for Quebecers, by Quebecers, who can now have access to a dentist anytime, anywhere from the comfort of their own home.

Something had to be done after March 16th, 2020 when the Quebec Order of Dentists and Public Health ordered the shutdown of dental clinics. It was hard for me to accept that I couldn't see my patients anymore.

They are the reason I love what I do. The reason I do my follow-ups personally is for that egotistical enjoyment of chatting with my patients and see what they were up since last time I saw them, how are their children, how was that new job interview, when are they moving in their new house?

That is also why we came up with weekly patient education group meetings, to keep in contact with them, make sure they are okay, being in front, so they know they can count on us if they need us.

And that's when I met Dr. Bak Nguyen, or actually, that's when I re-met him. In between conferences and symposiums, sometimes we know of someone because it is a small world, especially when you've been 16 years in practice.

So this crisis allowed me to reconnect with Dr. Bak, to see how engaged he is to save the profession, how much effort he put connecting people from all around the world to brainstorm an unprecedented industry's crisis, and that we had some similar questions, the most important being: how will dentistry be after COVID-19?

Of course, dentistry is and will remain a very hands-on profession, there is no doubt about that. Our relevancy is intrinsic to our unique talents as restorative artists, as surgeons of the oral cavity, as practitioners who connect the dots between the mouth and the whole body.

I firmly believe our communities will grow to become stronger when all of this settles down to the *"new normal"*. But that *"new normal"* needs to be defined, and it needs to be defined sooner than later by being proactive, asking the right questions and taking decisions on **evidence-based medicine rather than fear**.

I am blessed to love what I do, to be able to give back to our community through different initiatives of its leaders and some of our own and to contribute to the health of my community.

We can accomplish unbelievable wonders for patients nowadays. Who thought that they can have dental implants and teeth the same day? Who thought that their surgeries are performed virtually already before they even sit down at the appointment? I will never cease to be amazed by our profession. For that reason, dentistry will prevail, with some modifications and upgrades and in a different context, but it will prevail. And that is why we, as dentists, have to move forward.

They say that your job does not define who you are. It might be true. But what if your job is a passion that follows your every move, a passion so strong that when put up against the wall, that wall just disappears and new possibilities arise? Our vision at the office is to impact and change lives, one smile at a time. And that is what we will continue to do. Because… **WE ARE DENTISTS**.

This is how we will prevail. This is how we will all survive. This is how we will prosper, as one. This is **RELEVANCY**.

Dr. BAK NGUYEN

CHAPTER 27
"AN ALPHA"
by JONAS DIOP

My name is Jonas Diop, I am a performance coach and strategist. I want to share with you my quest journey. Everything start when I was just a kid, as some of us, I was introvert and of top of that, I am the youngest of the family, with one sister and two brothers.

My siblings and my mom had expectations. I just follow their rules and perspectives but at some point, I knew something was wrong, I knew that I was different.

I wasn't looking for fame, I wasn't looking for recognition. I wasn't seeking for money either. What I really wanted was to be happy. As I grew up, my mom had difficult times, she raised us only by her strong work ethic and values. She is a true leader and for not disappointed her, I just conform, seeking social recognition and everything else she wanted from and for me.

I was on this path, to be the good son, to attend university and to apply for a nice job and a house… I appreciated that stable vision but was not my destiny. I find my path to happiness in my improvement, in empowering others and in reaching new heights.

I started, like most of you, as a nobody. I was not important, that why I create my own legend. From nothing to something. My sister told me once: "If you face hard challenges, it's your chance to see your true character, what are you made of."

I went out and seek my destiny.

Step by step, I learn from mentors, peoples that impact the world, peoples who change the world on a daily basis. I started to read their biographies, to attend their classes, to reach them with my podcast about to become a conqueror. Yes, you can conquer your fears. Yes, you can conquer your dreams. Yes, you can conquer your life. One achiever after the next, I ask them their secret to success. Professional athletes, millionaires, CEO, etc...

All respect my hustle, but just a few give me leverage to achieve my purpose. One of them is Dr. Bak. A friend of mine introduced me to Dr. Bak, telling me about a man in a permanent state of momentum. My first sentence shaking Dr. Bak's hand was: "You have to be on my show, I need to interview you." His answer was a simple "Sure, let's do this."

A week later I was in front of him with all my gear to make one of the most powerful interviews that I ever realized. He surprised me with his sincerity, his heart and his pragmatism. He literally put himself at the same stage, at the same position as my audience to give them his perspective with an Alpha's confidence and an achiever's experience.

During these 45 minutes, we just connected and shared a good vibe. That's why I choose him to be my mentor, it's not about what he had already accomplished but more about what he will accomplish next. I wanted to be inspired and to learn from him his mindset and drive. We are in the same woods, we strive for challenges.

We started to share ideas, possibilities. Within the weeks and the months passing, we forged a bond, a friendship. Now, we are brothers.

Dr. Bak's kindness was to empower me to reveal myself, to be proud of who I am doing, to not see myself from the eyes of others. I heard that message a thousand time. But in his presence, I felt the true weight of each word. That changed my life.

Dr. Bak is a genius plain and simple. To me, he is also a superhero, with many extraordinary powers. I am telling you, the man has skills from another dimension! One thing, he is fast, very very fast. No one believes him when he says that he is writing a book within 2 weeks. People are looking for the lie and the catch. Well, I was there, more than once, and I saw the man in action.

Yes, he is writing himself, from his phone or his laptop. The man can write as quickly as he speaks, and believe me, he can talk fast and for a while… if you have his interest.

The most impressive is that he is doing it on top of his daily jobs as CEO and dentist… and that he keeps doing it, again and again. He is now at his 64th book! If that is not legend material, I don't know what is. It is something to read about power but to have the privilege to witness one in action is the chance of a lifetime!

I wanted a taste of his power. I managed to gain his attention and got an invite to join a book with him. We wrote that book in less a week, **MASTERMIND**, my first published book and his 52nd.

That's who he is, that's Dr. Bak. If he had something on his mind, he executes it as we are still speaking about the idea. Looking at him, it is effortless, frictionless and intoxicating. Dr. Bak is one of the smartest people that I know. But, his power and momentum are from his work ethic, even if he likes to label himself as lazy.

The quicker that you are to make a decision, the more you will minimize the risk of failure. It is not to have the right decision that counts, but to grow confidence to make that decision and to walk your talk. No time for regret, only to re-aim and to push until you've reached the finished line. And then, you move on. This is what I learned with Dr. Bak as a mentor.

He taught me that failure is not when you do not reach your goal, but failure is when you stop trying, you stop improving yourself. Working with him is a world of endless possibilities, it's a world of quickness and so much more. He is a mentor to me.

Imagine how moved I was when I read the passage where he is thanking me in public for my contribution to his success, showing him the art of podcasting, of interviewing. This is true gratitude and true humility, the traits of real leadership.

I am not a dentist, and yet, I am writing a chapter in what may come to redefine your profession. My advice to you is to feel Dr. Bak's words and find your inspiration to find your own path. He might have written more than 1 million words within 2 years and a half, but his words are all true, inspiring and genuine.

Right now on my sun quest journey's, I am happy. I found serenity as I am able to communicate my true essence in being myself, thanks to the helping hand of Dr.Bak

More than the **RELEVANCY** of your profession, with Dr. Bak leadership and influence, like me, you might find your identity and your happiness. Believe him when he is seeking happiness to those around him, even if he later wrapped those in words of **SUCCESS**, **MILLIONAIRE** and **QUESTS**. What keeps Dr. Bak relevant is his desire for happiness and his playfulness to push the boundaries.

He is a game-changer, I can tell so much but you need to discover that by yourself. With him by your side, I truly believe that you have not only the chance to survive this crisis but a true shot at redefining your kind to its rightful place.

Welcome to the **ALPHAS**, that's Dr. Bak embrace. Well, seize the day and be happy! You are an ALPHA!

This is how we will prevail. This is how we will all survive. This is how we will prosper, as one. This is **RELEVANCY**.

Dr. BAK NGUYEN

CONCLUSION
by Dr. BAK NGUYEN

This is TOME 2. The first one was written years ago, titled **PROFESSION HEALTH, the unconventional quest of happiness**. I was looking for answers and looking to understand why so many of us are subjects to depression and suicidal tendency. Now I know, it is because of the **VOID**, the one we do not talk about.

As I subtitled the first TOME 1 Diagnosis, this one is the plan of treatment, the course of action. Written with a different team and under completely different circumstances, I found my answer reaching out for strangers, people who will come to be called **THE ALPHAS**.

More than the quest for happiness, the unprecedented crisis of the **COVID WAR** brought me to seek something new: **RELEVANCY**. Not for myself, but for our profession, for our kind.

"For the first time of our lifetime, all interests aligned."
Dr. Bak Nguyen

This was true at the beginning of the war against the virus. That was two months ago. The **GREAT PAUSE** is not over yet, that the statement is starting to erode already. Within the new reality, many have found a new stability and normal, as hard as it may sound. Too quickly, all interests stopped their alignment, already.

Things are shifting very quickly, after the initial shock and denial, complacency has already begun to return to our beds. **Time is of essence here, speed is of essence!**

I know this is a conclusion, so I usually go back on the chapters, but it was too tempting to not bring a new card on the table. Yes, our relevancy fell to 3% or even less. Yes, the survival of our profession is at stake. Yes, this virus will kill much more than the official body count. Our entire way of life may be on the line.

The more I think of it, the more I can see how fragile our systems and society are. Just from a pause, a few weeks still and things started to crumble. Yes, I am talking about the economy, about the social order, about Life. Well, Life is dynamic. The Economy is dynamic and so is our society.

The reason why were are facing to lose so much in so little time is because we forgot how dynamic and interdependent our systems and society were. Now on pause, none of us is used to stand still, none of our systems and institution knows how to adapt.

> "Life is dynamic and so are our economy and society.
> Can we stop trying to define them in stone?"
> Dr. Bak Nguyen

Already, we see the infringements of freedom and individual rights. And with **FEAR**, things will just get worst from here. The ground and the decisions are shifting much faster than one can follow. This is our new reality, to all of us.

In the midst, how important is it to define our **RELEVANCY** as dentists? As professionals working in the health of the mouth? Well, if we do not awake right away and dwell on our purpose from the settled and crystallized **DUST OF COMPLACENCY**, we might never have the chance anymore, because there will be so many more important topics… even to each of us.

Make no mistake, we will see the light, we will survive, but will we be who we were, or much lesser? There is still a chance to be so much more and to live up to those dreams we had, entering the profession, years ago. Thank you Dr. Renafarje to remind us WHY we became dentists in the first place. But we need to awake and act, right now!

It is with hope and fortitude that I look at the future, believing in a better one, for all of us. Paul, my dear friend and co-author is leading the way, reinventing himself at 75 years old. He is as hopeful as a freshman fresh out of school! Thank you, Paul, for your wisdom, but also, for leading the way with such dignity, such inspiration. But we need to awake and act now!

> "In times of crisis, one has to reinvent oneself."
> Dr. Bak Nguyen

It is not every day that happiness comes served on a silver platter. Thank you, Anil, for your kindness and generosity. I would have said wisdom too, but the rule of literacy oblige me to vary my words. Thank you.

Forget 5G, it might kill you. The 3G will save your lives, all of our lives! To find relevancy for our kind, we must first find footing within our own lives first. But we need to awake and act now!

And what about the how? Paul, Paul Dominique, who did not care who you were offending, you kept pushing forward for solutions. From a depth analysis of our Economical systems and its flaws to turn back that laser beam of yours right back at us, you showed us the kind of decision we will need to face to keep perfecting ourselves, to keep our relevancy.

Honestly, from 3%, how lower can it gets? Well, much lower if we do not see the truth and the message written on the wall. Thank you, Paul Dominique, for your fortitude and… yes, wisdom! But we need to awake and act now!

> "For a new world dialogue, not a new world order!"
> Dr. Bak Nguyen

Aren't we all looking for purpose? We were, and yet, we got stuck at the glass ceiling, one we made from out of our need for differentiation, for competition. With the Tsunami hitting, the flood will clean everything below sea level... in plain words, the relevancy level. But we will act to act now and to act fast!

> "The Tsunami will clean everything below sea level...
> in plain words, the relevancy level."
> Dr. Bak Nguyen

We have a way to the other side if we have the heart to embrace it. The **OUELLETTE INITIATIVE** is the bridge to safer grounds, but then, we will still need to understand how to rebuild. Eric, you summarized this quest so eloquently. And then, Duc, you remind us what we are in the eye of the public. Thank you. But we need to awake and act now!

From expanding our market shares to helping those in needs, writing this book proved that left and right can come together to build from the differences. I am from the corporate and finance side, and yet I got along with Eric, a community leader to bridge the **VOID**, the one left since dental school.

Nach raised the need for quality of care, for technology and for how fast we could embrace and leverage them to get out of this mess. You shared openly how quickly you have adapted in the past to redefine yourself. You never met nor even exchange with Paul Ouellette, and yet, we can find the same attribute to success, the same vision of hope. Thank you. But we need to awake and act now!

> "To be flexible, humble and to keep adapting."
> Christian Trudeau

I've borrowed inspiration from the people I knew and those I reached out for and never met. From coast to coast, from one ocean to the next, it is so strange how we could agree on the diagnosis of our pain and situation. Now, can we agree as swiftly on the course of actions and the direction moving forward? How hard can that be, it is forward!?!

> "To build from the difference."
> Dr. Jean De Serres

I finished the last paragraphs with quotes from my mentors, Christian Trudeau who led the age of digitalization from its dawn and Dr. Jean De Serres who led health organization and pharmaceutical researches bridging the future of medicine.

Well, we all agree on the how and the why, along with all the **ALPHAS** on board. And still, we need to all move together, this time, there is no first or last, only those who have made it and those who will be forgotten… and if too many are forgotten, those who made it will simply be assimilated into a stronger group.

Are we ready to disappear? Are we ready to be assimilated? We are still holding upon our **3% relevancy**! But we need to awake and act now!

For those who know me. For those who read me, I am nothing but hope and positivity. But I found it too important to leave aside the **urgency of the situation**. I am not advocating for a revolution, but a fast evolution, one where nothing is safe from the upgrades and the change. One free from the pride of the lies of perfection, one humble and one that can keep enough flexibility to adapt quickly.

I believe because Paul, at 75 believes. I believe because, just like Eric, I won't die before making sure of my relevancy. I have hope because Paul Dominique had the fortitude to defy the establishment and complacency to share a remedy to build, once on the other side.

I know that we can build from our difference if people like Nach, Eric and I can share the same platform and build constructively, from our difference, with respect and having much fun doing so. Yes, we are all **ALPHAS**, with egos and big personalities, but that didn't come in the way. We leveraged them to gap the **VOID**.

I believe, I hope and I am holding the ground, the passage to the outside with the help of my friends and peers, of my companions, the **ALPHAS**. What about you? The choice is yours, but time isn't on your side.

This is not the end, but the beginning of a long journey. If just like every great story ever told, there are 3 acts, **THE VOID AND THE AWAKENING** is act 1. The passing of the **BRIDGE** is act 2. And the **REBUILDING** is act 3.

In the framework of most legends, act 2 and 3 are the most brutal and challenging. Will that be our case, in our quest for our **RELEVANCY?** You seem to have forgotten one crucial element.

We are dentists, from the elite. We are chosen and trained to be resilient and to go beyond what is asked of us. Well, this time the test is to raise our **RELEVANCY** to numbers we usually accepted as normal, above average!

If we awake now and act as one, we are stronger than the past told us we are; much more than the authorities will like us to believe. Our battle is not against any of them but against our complacency and our beliefs.

We are what we think. Look up and you'll be moving up. Look down, well... 3G, **Give, Gratitude and Grow**. Giving is empowering. To be grateful is to recognize our needs and to be appreciative of our assets. Lightness will come from giving as humility from gratitude. Then, growing is not even a step, it becomes a consequence!

Imagine that kind of power within hands like ours! Imagine the difference we can make if we, the elite, all act as one, building over the glass ceiling that enslaved us for too long!

Just like me, open up and you won't have to walk alone, not anymore. Just like I found in Paul, Christian and Jean, a way to learn from their past the blueprint to build my future, our future, you too, can be part of the dialogue and the solution.

Just like me, you will find friends and peers like I found in Eric and Nach, Paul Dominique and Anil to build from the difference with much fun. Just like me, you will expand your horizon and potential, like I did with Julio, Duc, Martin and Jonas. Building from our difference, challenging and inspiring each other to always surpass ourselves.

Don't overachieve, that's a side effect, looking back. To borrow the word of my Alpha Friend, Dr. Nach Daniel, overseek and keep doing so!

In the past, we did that to prove who was the best. Now, we do it out of habit. Not the beat the other guy, but to build the step on which he will jump from until, at our turn, we'll be jumping from his shoulder.

Together, this is how we have built bridges and solutions out of thin air. The future is ours to embrace, ours to make and ours to build, upon our **RELEVANCY**.

This is how we will prevail. This is how we will all survive. This is how we will prosper, as one. This is **RELEVANCY**.

I am Dr. Bak, welcome to **THE ALPHAS**.

Dr. BAK NGUYEN

RELEVANCY

by LINKED IN AND TOWN HALL ACHIEVER OF THE YEAR
EY NOMINEE ENTREPRENEUR OF THE YEAR
GRAND HOMAGE LYS DIVERSITY
Dr. BAK NGUYEN, DMD

&

by TWO TIMES LAUREATE ICOI WORLD CONGRESS TOP PRESENTER
WORLD'S TOP 100 DOCTORS IN DENTISTRY
Dr. PAUL OUELLETTE, DDS, MS, ABO, AFAAID

guest authors

Dr. ANIL GUPTA
Dr. PAUL DOMINIQUE
Dr. ERIC LACOSTE

Dr. NACH DANIEL
Dr. JULIO CESAR REYNAFARJE
Dr. MARIA KUNSTADTER
Dr. DUC-MINH LAM-DO
Dr. JEREMY KRELL
Dr. AGATHA BIS

MARTIN LAVALLÉE
ALIA ALAOUI
JONAS DIOP

ABOUT THE AUTHORS

From Canada, **Dr Bak Nguyen**, Nominee EY Entrepreneur of the year, Grand Homage LYS DIVERSITY, and LinkedIn & TownHall Achiever of the year. Dr Bak is a cosmetic dentist, CEO and founder of Mdex & Co. His company is revolutionizing the dental field. Speaker and motivator, he wrote more than 65 books in 2 years and a half, accumulating many world records (to be officialized).

From USA: **Dr. Paul Ouellette**, DDS, MS, ABO, AFAAID, WORLD TOP 100 DENTISTS, Former Associate Professor Georgia School of Orthodontics and Jacksonville University. A visionary man looking for the future of our profession. Dr. Paul Ouellette Highly motivated to help my sons become successful in the "Ouellette Family of Dentists" Group Dental Specialty Practice.

GUEST AUTHORS

From USA: **Dr. Anil Gupta** is a world-class speaker and coach helping people to find their purpose and happiness. Dr. Gupta is in the quest to improve one billion lives throughout the world. A man of wisdom, a kind force of nature and a motivator spreading hope.

From USA, **Dr. Paul Dominique** is a pediatric dentist who joined the profession at 27 years old. From public dental health, he moved on to build a network of clinics and sold them a few years back. Now, at 49, he is half retired and is investing in different dental tech companies, including teledentistry.

From Canada, **Dr Eric Lacoste**, Periodontist and MBA, Dr Lacoste is a community leader and great entrepreneur who is fighting for the weakest links of our society, especially children. Twice DUNAMIS laureate, HOMAGE from the Quebec Dentists Order and winner of the TELUS Social Implication Award.

From Canada, **Dr. Nach Daniel** is an Oral & Maxillofacial Surgeon and successful businessman with more than 300 employees in his dental company, EAST COAST DENTAL GROUP. Dr. Daniel has a diverse portfolio ranging from commercial real estate to AI.

From USA, **Dr. Maria Kunstadter**, Doctor of Dental Surgery, co-founder THE TELEDENTIST, the biggest TELEDENTISTRY provider in USA. Experienced President with a demonstrated history of working in the hospital & health care industry. Skilled in Customer Service, Sales, Strategic Planning, Team Building, and Public Speaking. Strong business development professional with a Doctor of Dental Surgery focused in Advanced General Dentistry from UMKC School of Dentistry.

From Peru: **Dr. Julio Reynafarje**, dentist, Dean of the Peruvian Dental Association postgraduate School of continued Education. Postgraduate professor for more than 15 years, with more than 100 international lectures and with publications in many languages in magazines worldwide, he is also the author of the book Sfumato in Esthetic dentistry and is an active entrepreneur in Medical issues.

From Canada, **Dr Duc-Minh Lam-Do**, dentist for 16 years with a practice emphasis on functional and physiologic dentistry, co-founder of teledentistes.com, the first teledentistry platform in Quebec. He is the founder of the Montreal Tongue-tie Institute, the first comprehensive multidisciplinary center for the treatment of ankyloglossia for babies, children and adults who have issues related with breastfeeding, swallowing, breathing, speech and craniofacial growth. He is one of 6 dentists in Quebec who has a mastership from the American Academy of Dental Sleep Medicine.

From USA, **Dr Jeremy Krell**, dentist MBA and serial entrepreneur, the real definition of an OVERACHIEVER. Highly experienced innovator and entrepreneur with a proven track record of taking early-stage startups to acquisition (multi-million dollar buyout). Excellent clinical dentistry and communication skills with in-depth analytical, organizational, and problem-solving abilities. A detail orientated and strategic leader in a dynamic, expeditious innovative environment. Firm experience with strategy, positioning companies, leading & developing teams, raising capital, investor relations, dental materials & techniques, negotiating & closing deals, and sales.

From Canada, **Dr. Agatha Bis**, dentist for 20 years+, founder of UPB Dental Academy.

From Canada: **Martin Lavallée, MBA**, and CEO of the INSTITUT DENTAIRE INTERNATIONAL (I.D.I) dedicated to accompany and support with continuous education the dentists on their journey to excel.

From Canada: **Alia Alaoui,** CEO of SWIPELIST Inc., Artificial intelligence marketplace that connects patients with dentists

From France, **Jonas Diop**, coach and podcaster, Jonas is the voice of a new generation, one refusing to bow down to anything less than life to the fullest. Entrepreneur and businessman, his passion is to empower the dreamer within each individual to become achievers. From dreamer to achiever!

ULTIMATE AUDIO EXPERIENCE

A new way to learn and enjoy Audiobooks. Made to be entertaining while keeping the self-educational value of a book, UAX will appeal to both auditive and visual people. UAX is the blockbuster of the Audiobooks.

UAX will cover most of Dr Bak's books, and is now negotiating to bring more authors and more titles to the UAX concept. Now streaming on Spotify, Apple Music and available for download on all major music platforms. Give it a try today!

www.DrBakNguyen.com

AMAZON - APPLE BOOKS - KINDLE - SPOTIFY - APPLE MUSIC

FROM THE SAME AUTHOR
Dr Bak Nguyen

www.DrBakNguyen.com

MAJOR LEAGUES' ACCESS

FACTEUR HUMAIN -032
LE LEADERSHIP DU SUCCÈS
par DR BAK NGUYEN & CHRISTIAN TRUDEAU

ehappyPedia -037
THE RISE OF THE UNICORN
BY Dr BAK NGUYEN & Dr JEAN DE SERRES

CHAMPION MINDSET -038
LEARNING TO WIN
BY Dr BAK NGUYEN & CHRISTOPHE MULUMBA

BRANDING DrBAK -039
BALANCING STRATEGY AND EMOTIONS
BY Dr BAK NGUYEN

BUSINESS

SYMPHONY OF SKILLS -001
BY Dr BAK NGUYEN

La Symphonie des Sens -002
ENTREPREUNARIAT
par DR BAK NGUYEN

INDUSTRIES DISRUPTORS -006
BY Dr BAK NGUYEN

CHANGING THE WORLD FROM A DENTAL CHAIR -007
BY Dr BAK NGUYEN

SELFMADE -035
GRATITUDE AND HUMILITY
BY Dr BAK NGUYEN

CHILDREN'S BOOK
with William Bak

The Trilogy of Legends

THE LEGEND OF THE CHICKEN HEART -016
LA LÉGENDE DU COEUR DE POULET -017
BY Dr BAK NGUYEN & WILLIAM BAK

THE LEGEND OF THE LION HEART -018
LA LÉGENDE DU COEUR DE LION -019
BY Dr BAK NGUYEN & WILLIAM BAK

THE LEGEND OF THE DRAGON HEART -020
LA LÉGENDE DU COEUR DE DRAGON -021
BY Dr BAK NGUYEN & WILLIAM BAK

WE ARE ALL DRAGONS -022
NOUS TOUS, DRAGONS -023
BY Dr BAK NGUYEN & WILLIAM BAK

THE 9 SECRETS OF THE SMART CHICKEN -025
LES 9 SECRETS DU POULET INTELLIGENT -026
BY Dr BAK NGUYEN & WILLIAM BAK

THE SECRET OF THE FAST CHICKEN -027
LE SECRETS DU POULET RAPIDE -028
BY Dr BAK NGUYEN & WILLIAM BAK

THE LEGEND OF THE SUPER CHICKEN -029
LA LÉGENDE DU SUPER POULET -030
BY Dr BAK NGUYEN & WILLIAM BAK

THE STORY OF THE CHICKEN SHIT -031
L'HISTOIRE DU CACA DE POULET -032
BY Dr BAK NGUYEN & WILLIAM BAK

WHY CHICKEN CAN'T DREAM? -033
POURQUOI LES POULETS NE RÊVENT PAS? -034
BY Dr BAK NGUYEN & WILLIAM BAK

THE STORY OF THE CHICKEN NUGGET -057
BY Dr BAK NGUYEN & WILLIAM BAK

DENTISTRY

PROFESSION HEALTH - TOME ONE -005
THE UNCONVENTIONAL QUEST OF HAPPINESS
BY Dr BAK NGUYEN, Dr MIRJANA SINDOLIC,
Dr ROBERT DURAND AND COLLABORATORS

HOW TO NOT FAIL AS A DENTIST -046
BY Dr BAK NGUYEN

SUCCESS IS A CHOICE -060
BLUEPRINTS FOR HEALTH PROFESSIONALS
BY Dr BAK NGUYEN

RELEVANCY - TOME TWO -064
REINVENTING OURSELVES TO SURVIVE
BY Dr BAK NGUYEN & Dr PAUL OUELLETTE AND COLLABORATORS

MIDAS TOUCH -065
POST-COVID DENTISTRY
BY Dr BAK NGUYEN, Dr JULIO REYNAFARJE AND Dr PAUL OUELLETTE

THE POWER OF DR -066
THE MODERN TITLE OF NOBILITY
BY Dr BAK NGUYEN, Dr KIANOR SHAH AND COLLABORATORS

QUEST OF IDENTITY

IDENTITY -004
THE ANTHOLOGY OF QUESTS
BY Dr BAK NGUYEN

HYBRID -011
THE MODERN QUEST OF IDENTITY
BY Dr BAK NGUYEN

FORCES OF NATURE -015
FORGING THE CHARACTER OF WINNERS
BY Dr BAK NGUYEN

LIFESTYLE

HORIZON, BUILDING UP THE VISION -045
VOLUME ONE
BY Dr BAK NGUYEN

HORIZON, ON THE FOOTSTEP OF TITANS -047
VOLUME TWO
BY Dr BAK NGUYEN

HORIZON, DREAMING OF TRAVELING -068
VOLUME THREE
BY Dr BAK NGUYEN

MILLION DOLLAR MINDSET

MOMENTUM TRANSFER -009
BY Dr BAK NGUYEN & Coach DINO MASSON

MENTORS -010
BY Dr BAK NGUYEN

LEVERAGE -014
COMMUNICATION INTO SUCCESS
BY Dr BAK NGUYEN AND COLLABORATORS

THE POWER OF YES -016
MY 18 MONTHS JOURNEY
BY Dr BAK NGUYEN

HOW TO WRITE A BOOK IN 30 DAYS -040
BY Dr BAK NGUYEN

POWER -042
EMOTIONAL INTELLIGENCE
BY Dr BAK NGUYEN

HOW TO WRITE A SUCCESSFUL BUSINESS PLAN -048
BY Dr BAK NGUYEN & ROUBA SAKR

MINDSET ARMORY -049
BY Dr BAK NGUYEN

MASTERMIND, 7 WAYS INTO THE BIG LEAGUE -052
BY Dr BAK NGUYEN & JONAS DIOP

PLAYBOOK INTRODUCTION -055
BY Dr BAK NGUYEN

PLAYBOOK INTRODUCTION 2 -056
BY Dr BAK NGUYEN

RISING -062
TO WIN MORE THAN YOU ARE AFRAID TO LOSE
BY Dr BAK NGUYEN

TORNADO -067
FORCE OF CHANGE
BY Dr BAK NGUYEN

PARENTING

THE BOOK OF LEGENDS -024
BY Dr BAK NGUYEN & WILLIAM BAK

THE BOOK OF LEGENDS 2 -041
BY Dr BAK NGUYEN & WILLIAM BAK

THE BOOK OF LEGENDS 3 -051
THE END OF THE INNOCENCE AGE
BY Dr BAK NGUYEN & WILLIAM BAK

PERSONAL GROWTH

REBOOT -012
MIDLIFE CRISIS
BY Dr BAK NGUYEN

HUMILITY FOR SUCCESS -050
BALANCING STRATEGY AND EMOTIONS
BY Dr BAK NGUYEN

THE ENERGY FORMULA -053
BY Dr BAK NGUYEN

AMONGST THE ALPHA -058
BY Dr BAK NGUYEN & COACH JONAS DIOP

AMONGST THE ALPHA vol.2 -059
ON THE OTHER SIDE
BY Dr BAK NGUYEN & COACH JONAS DIOP

THE 90 DAYS CHALLENGE -061
BY Dr BAK NGUYEN

THE MODERN WOMAN -070
TO HAVE IT HAVE WITH NO SACRIFICE
BY Dr BAK NGUYEN & Dr EMILY LETRAN

EMPORWERMENT -069
I DO IT FOR YOU, I DO IT FOR ME
BY Dr BAK NGUYEN

PHILOSOPHY

LEADERSHIP -003
PANDORA'S BOX
BY Dr BAK NGUYEN

KRYPTO -043
TO SAVE THE WORLD
BY Dr BAK NGUYEN & ILYAS BAKOUCH

SOCIETY

LE RÊVE CANADIEN -013
D'IMMIGRANT À MILLIONNAIRE
par DR BAK NGUYEN

CHOC -054
LE JARDIN D'EDITH
par DR BAK NGUYEN

AFTERMATH -063
BUSINESS AFTER THE GREAT PAUSE
BY Dr BAK NGUYEN & Dr ERIC LACOSTE

WOMAN EMPOWERMENT

THE POWER BEHIND THE ALPHA -008
BY TRANIE VO & Dr BAK NGUYEN

THE MODERN WOMAN -070
TO HAVE IT ALL WITH NO SACRIFICE
Dr BAK NGUYEN & Dr Emily LETRAN

www.DrBakNguyen.com

AMAZON - APPLE BOOKS - KINDLE - SPOTIFY - APPLE MUSIC

www.ingramcontent.com/pod-product-compliance
Lightning Source LLC
Chambersburg PA
CBHW060941230426
43665CB00015B/2023